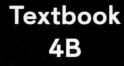

**Textbook
4B**

Maths —
No Problem!

Singapore Maths
English National Curriculum 2014

Consultant and Author
Dr. Yeap Ban Har

UK Consultant
Dr. Anne Hermanson

MATHS
NO PROBLEM!

shinglee

Published by Maths — No Problem!
Copyright © 2017 by Maths — No Problem!

Printed in the United Kingdom
First Printing, 2015
Reprinted once in 2016 and once in 2017

ISBN 978-1-910504-18-5

Maths — No Problem!
Dowding House, Coach & Horses Passage
Tunbridge Wells, UK TN2 5NP
www.mathsnoproblem.co.uk

Acknowledgements

This Maths — No Problem! series, adapted from the New Syllabus
Primary Mathematics series, is published in collaboration with
Shing Lee Publishers. Pte Ltd. The publisher would like to thank
Dr. Tony Gardiner for his contribution.

Design and Illustration by Kin

Preface

Maths — No Problem! is a comprehensive series that adopts a spiral design with carefully built-up mathematical concepts and processes adapted from the maths mastery approaches used in Singapore. The Concrete-Pictorial-Abstract (C-P-A) approach forms an integral part of the learning process through the materials developed for this series.

Maths — No Problem! incorporates the use of concrete aids and manipulatives, problem-solving and group work.

In Maths — No Problem! Primary 4, these features are exemplified throughout the chapters:

Chapter Opener

Familiar events or occurrences that serve as an introduction for pupils.

In Focus

Includes questions related to various lesson objectives as an introductory activity for pupils.

Let's Learn

Introduces new concepts through a C-P-A approach with the use of engaging pictures and manipulatives. Guided examples are provided for reinforcement.

Activity Time

Provides pupils with opportunities to work as individuals or in small groups to explore mathematical concepts or to play games.

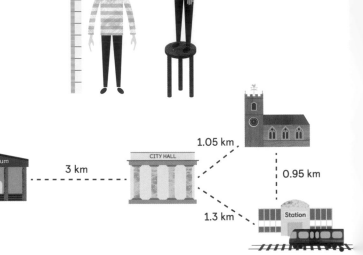

Guided Practice

Comprises questions for further consolidation and for the immediate evaluation of pupils' learning.

Mind Workout

Challenging non-routine questions for pupils to apply relevant heuristics and to develop higher-order thinking skills.

Treats
£1.55 for 1
Any 2 for £2.50
Any 3 for £3.25

Maths Journal

Provides pupils with opportunities to show their understanding of the mathematical concepts learnt.

Self Check

Allows pupils to assess their own learning after each chapter.

Self Check

I know how to...

☐ read and write Roman numerals for 1 to 20.

☐ read and write Roman numerals to 100.

Contents

Chapter 9	Money	Page

Chapter 10	Mass, Volume and Length	

		Page
Chapter 11	**Area of Figures**	

Chapter 12	**Geometry**

Chapter 13	Position and Movement	Page

Chapter 14	Roman Numerals	

Chapter 8
Decimals

Writing Tenths

In Focus

Look at the two numbers shown by the parts shaded in pink. How are they related?

This stands for 1.

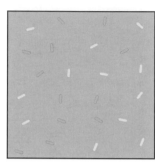

What does this stand for?

Let's Learn

1 Divide 1 into 10 equal parts.

 = 1

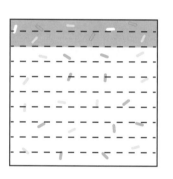 = 1 tenth

$$1 \text{ tenth} = \frac{1}{10} = 0.1$$

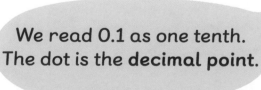
We read 0.1 as one tenth. The dot is the **decimal point**.

$\frac{1}{10}$ is 0.1 when written as a decimal.

2 Compare 0.1 and 1.

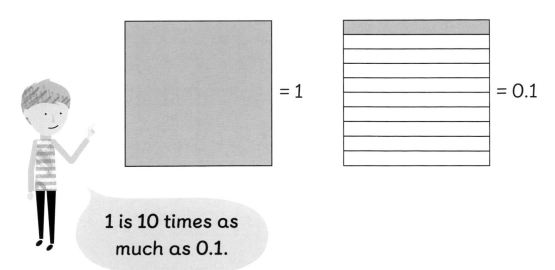

= 1   = 0.1

1 is 10 times as much as 0.1.

3 Write the number represented in each diagram as a decimal.

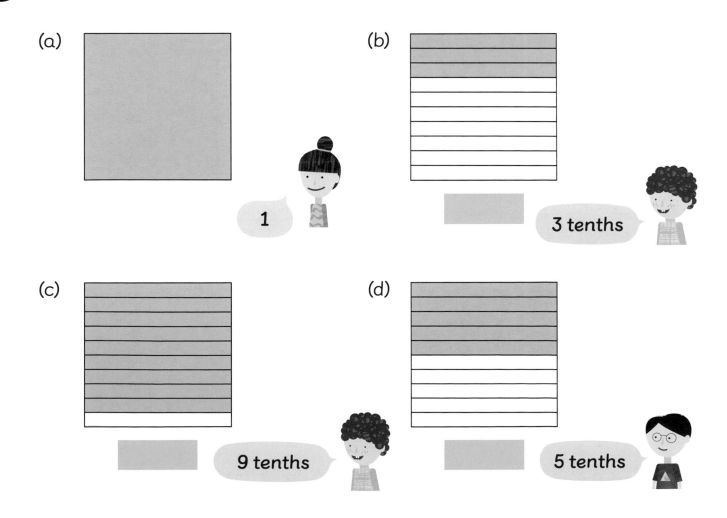

(a)

1

(b)

3 tenths

(c)

9 tenths

(d)

5 tenths

Guided Practice

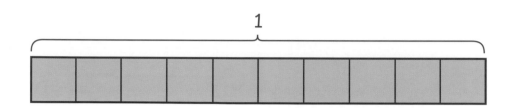

1

Write each number shown by the shaded part as a decimal.

(a)

(b)

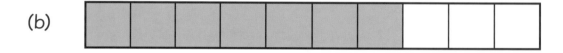

(c)

Complete Worksheet **1** – Page **1** - **2**

Writing Tenths

In Focus

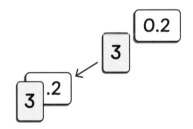

Let each ⬤ stand for either **1** or (0.1).

Use all ⬤⬤⬤⬤⬤ to make a number.

Let's Learn

1 makes **1** **1** **1** (0.1) (0.1).

ones	tenths
3	2

3 ones + 2 tenths

= 3 + 0.2

= 3.2

We read 3.2 as three and two tenths.

The digit 3 is in the ones place.

The digit 2 is in the tenths place.

2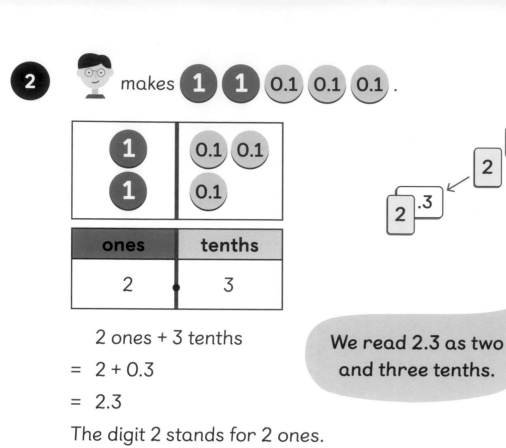

makes **1** **1** **0.1** **0.1** **0.1** .

ones	tenths
2	3

2 ones + 3 tenths

= 2 + 0.3

= 2.3

The digit 2 stands for 2 ones.

The digit 3 stand for 3 tenths.

We read 2.3 as two and three tenths.

3 makes **1** **0.1** **0.1** **0.1** **0.1** .

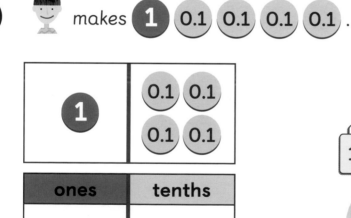

ones	tenths
1	4

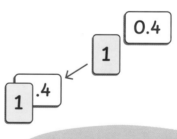

We read 1.4 as one and four tenths.

How many numbers can be made using ⬤ ⬤ ⬤ ⬤ ⬤ ?

What if there are ⬤ ⬤ ⬤ ⬤ instead?

Guided Practice

1 Use  to show each number .

(a) 1.6

(b) 2.4

(c) 4.8

(d) 0.3

2 What value does the digit 7 stand for in each number?

(a) 7.2

(b) 2.7

3

Let each ⬤ stand for either **1** or (0.1).

⬤⬤⬤⬤⬤⬤ can stand for 6 different numbers.

Explain if this is true.

Complete Worksheet 2 – Page 3 – 4

Writing Tenths

In Focus

Who is correct?

I use 3 counters to show 1.2.

I use 12 counters to show 1.2.

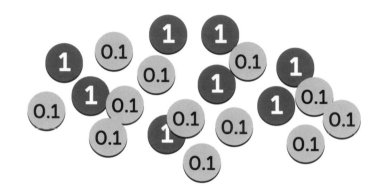

Let's Learn

 1 uses **1** **0.1** **0.1** to show 1.2.

ones	tenths
1	2

We read 1.2 as one and two tenths.

1.2

0   0.5   1   1.5   2

2 uses  to

show 1.2.

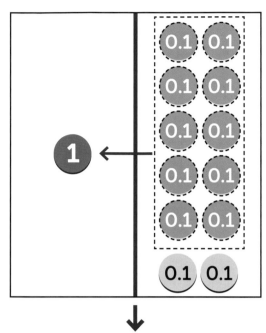

ones	tenths
1	2

12 tenths = 10 tenths + 2 tenths

= 1 one + 2 tenths

= 1.2

12 tenths = $\dfrac{12}{10}$

Guided Practice

1 Write each number as a decimal. Use 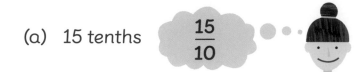 to help you.

(a) 15 tenths $\frac{15}{10}$

(b) 22 tenths $\frac{22}{10}$

(c) $\frac{30}{10}$

(d) $\frac{65}{10}$

2 What is the decimal represented by each letter?

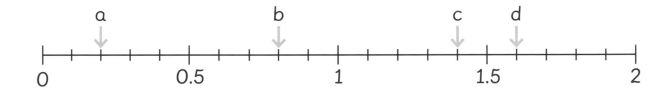

Writing Hundredths

In Focus

This stands for 1.

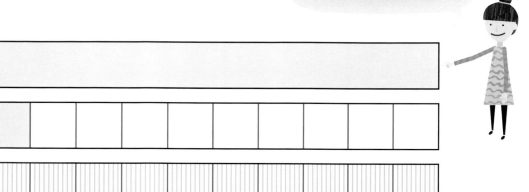

What number does each shaded part stand for?

Let's Learn

1 Divide 1 into 10 equal parts.

= 1

= 1 tenth

1 tenth = $\frac{1}{10}$ = 0.1

$\frac{1}{10}$ is 0.1 when written as a decimal.

2 Divide 1 into 100 equal parts.

= 1

= 1 hundredth

$$1 \text{ hundredth} = \frac{1}{100} = 0.01$$

$\frac{1}{100}$ is 0.01 when written as a decimal.

We read 0.01 as one hundredth.

3 What does each shaded part stand for?

(a)

$$\frac{8}{100} = 8 \text{ hundredths}$$

$$=$$

(b)

 $=$

How do you read this number?

How do you write this number?

4 The shaded part stands for ▭ .

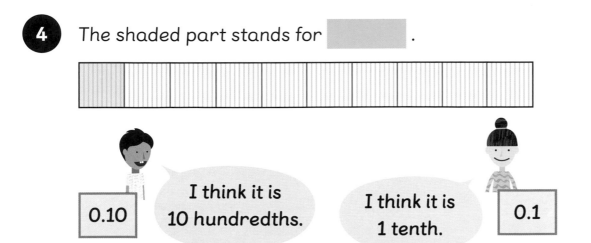

0.10 I think it is 10 hundredths. I think it is 1 tenth. 0.1

Who is correct?

Guided Practice

Write the decimal number shown by each shaded part.

1

(a) ▭

(b) ▭

(c) ▭

Read each of the numbers.

Complete Worksheet **4** – Page **7 – 8**

Writing Hundredths

In Focus

Miss Meharg designed an interesting kitchen scale.

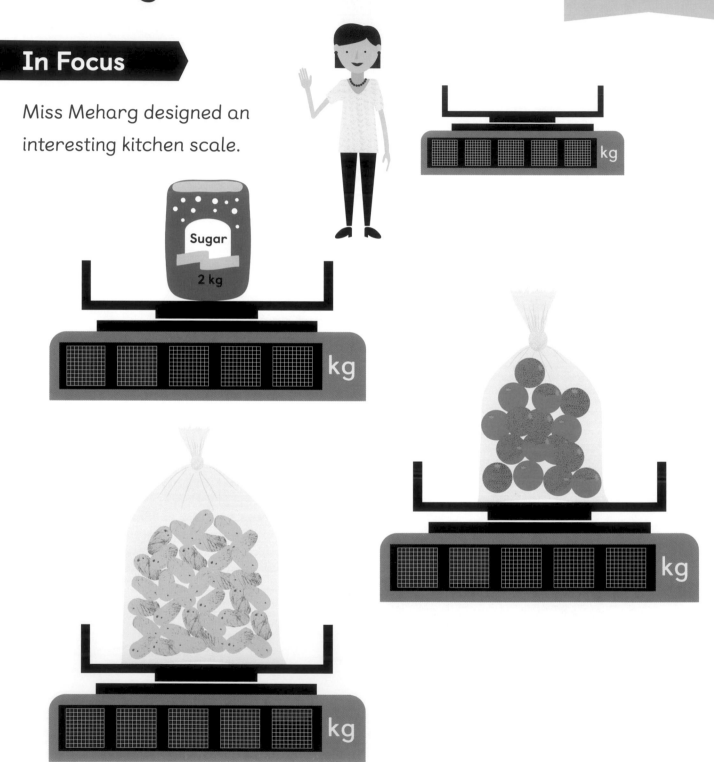

What is the mass shown on each scale?

Let's Learn

1

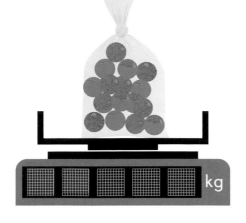

How many ?   1 one

How many ━━━━ ?   9 tenths

How many ▪ ?   0 hundredth

1.9 is read as one and nine tenths.

It shows 1.9 kg.

2

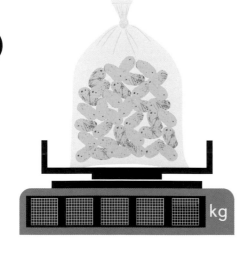

How many ?   4 ones

How many ━━━━ ?   2 tenths

How many ▪ ?   9 hundredths

4.29 is read as four and twenty-nine hundredths.

It shows 4.29 kg.

Guided Practice

1 Write and read the numbers shown on the scale.

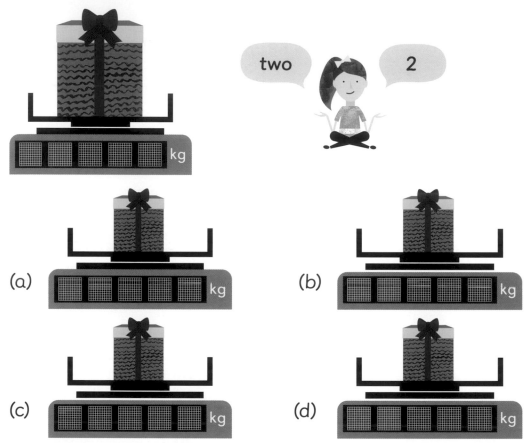

two   2

(a)   kg

(b)   kg

(c)   kg

(d)   kg

2 Show each number using 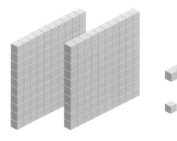 .

This shows 2.13.

(a)   1.3

(b)   0.13

(c)   1.03

Complete Worksheet **5** – Page **9 – 10**

Writing Hundredths

In Focus

What number does this show?

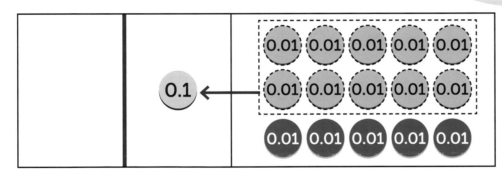

Let's Learn

1 15 hundredths = ▭

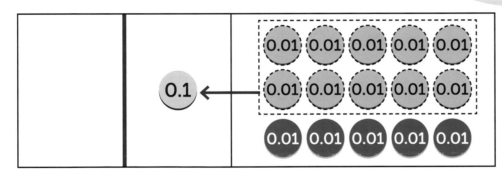

> Exchange 10 hundredths for 1 tenth.

ones	tenths	hundredths
0	1	5

15 hundredths = 10 hundredths + 5 hundredths

      = 1 tenth + 5 hundredths

      = 0.1 + 0.05

      = 0.15

> We read 0.15 as fifteen hundredths.

> We also read it as $\frac{15}{100}$.

The digit 1 is in the tenths place.

The digit 5 is in the hundredths place.

2 Write $1\frac{41}{100}$ as a decimal.

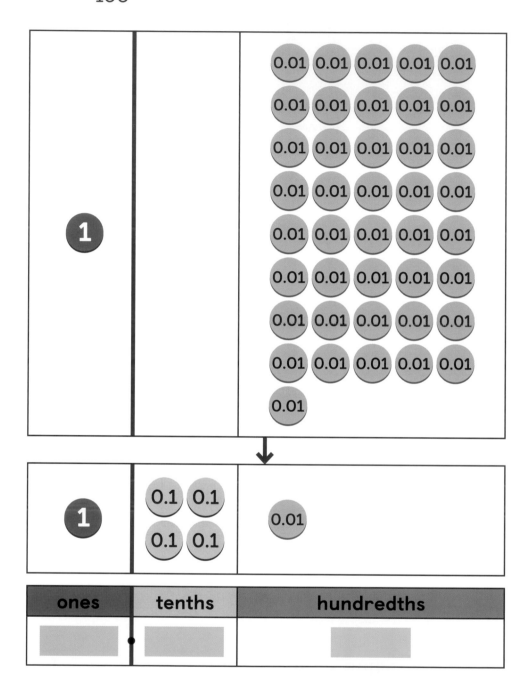

$$1\frac{41}{100} = \text{1 one + 4 tenths + 1 hundredth}$$
$$= 1 + 0.4 + 0.01$$
$$= 1.41$$

Guided Practice

1 Write each number as a decimal. Use ①, ⓪·1 and ⓪·01 to help you.

(a)   9 hundredths

(b)   68 hundredths

(c) $\dfrac{13}{100}$

(d) $\dfrac{99}{100}$

2 Write each number as a decimal. Use ①, ⓪·1 and ⓪·01 to help you.

(a) $2\dfrac{5}{100}$

(b) $2\dfrac{23}{100}$

(c) $4\dfrac{30}{100}$

(d) $1\dfrac{51}{100}$

3 Each ⚪ is either ⓪·1 or ⓪·01 .

How many different numbers could these ⚪ stand for?

Complete Worksheet 6 – Page 11 – 13

Writing Hundredths

In Focus

I use 124 0.01 to show a number.

What number is showing?
Can she use fewer discs
to show the same number?

0.01 0.01 0.01 0.01 0.01 0.01 0.01 0.01 0.01 0.01
0.01 0.01 0.01 0.01 0.01 0.01 0.01 0.01 0.01 0.01
0.01 0.01 0.01 0.01 0.01 0.01 0.01 0.01 0.01 0.01
0.01 0.01 0.01 0.01 0.01 0.01 0.01 0.01 0.01 0.01
0.01 0.01 0.01 0.01 0.01 0.01 0.01 0.01 0.01 0.01
0.01 0.01 0.01 0.01 0.01 0.01 0.01 0.01 0.01 0.01
0.01 0.01 0.01 0.01 0.01 0.01 0.01 0.01 0.01 0.01
0.01 0.01 0.01 0.01 0.01 0.01 0.01 0.01 0.01 0.01
0.01 0.01 0.01 0.01 0.01 0.01 0.01 0.01 0.01 0.01
0.01 0.01 0.01 0.01 0.01 0.01 0.01 0.01 0.01 0.01
0.01 0.01 0.01 0.01 0.01 0.01 0.01 0.01 0.01 0.01
0.01 0.01 0.01 0.01 0.01 0.01 0.01 0.01 0.01 0.01
0.01 0.01 0.01 0.01

1 uses (0.1) and (0.01) .

10 hundredths = 1 tenth

0.01	0.01	0.01	0.01	0.01	0.01	0.01	0.01	0.01	0.01		0.1
0.01	0.01	0.01	0.01	0.01	0.01	0.01	0.01	0.01	0.01		0.1
0.01	0.01	0.01	0.01	0.01	0.01	0.01	0.01	0.01	0.01		0.1
0.01	0.01	0.01	0.01	0.01	0.01	0.01	0.01	0.01	0.01		0.1
0.01	0.01	0.01	0.01	0.01	0.01	0.01	0.01	0.01	0.01		0.1
0.01	0.01	0.01	0.01	0.01	0.01	0.01	0.01	0.01	0.01		0.1
0.01	0.01	0.01	0.01	0.01	0.01	0.01	0.01	0.01	0.01	→	0.1
0.01	0.01	0.01	0.01	0.01	0.01	0.01	0.01	0.01	0.01		0.1
0.01	0.01	0.01	0.01	0.01	0.01	0.01	0.01	0.01	0.01		0.1
0.01	0.01	0.01	0.01	0.01	0.01	0.01	0.01	0.01	0.01		0.1
0.01	0.01	0.01	0.01	0.01	0.01	0.01	0.01	0.01	0.01		0.1
0.01	0.01	0.01	0.01	0.01	0.01	0.01	0.01	0.01	0.01		0.1

0.01 0.01 0.01 0.01   0.01 0.01 0.01 0.01

124 hundredths = 12 tenths + 4 hundredths

$$\frac{124}{100}$$

2 uses **1** and **0.01** .

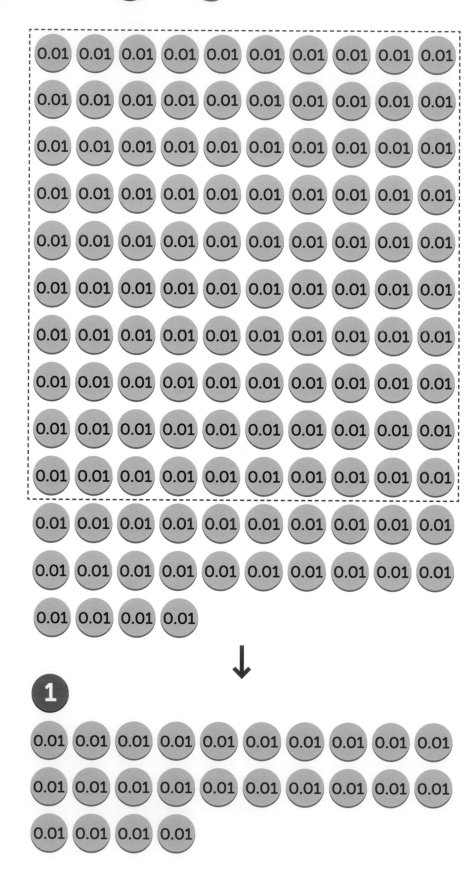

124 hundredths = 1 one + 24 hundredths

                = 1.24

We read 1.24 as one and twenty-four hundredths.

We also write it as $1\frac{24}{100}$.

The digit 1 is in the ones place

The digit 2 is in the tenths place.

The digit 4 is in the hundredths place.

1.24

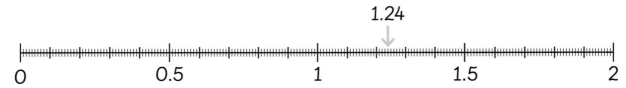

0   0.5   1   1.5   2

3 👧 uses (**1**) , (**0.1**) and (**0.01**) .

124 hundredths = 1 one + 2 tenths + 4 hundredths

ones	tenths	hundredths
1	2	4

Guided Practice

1 Write each number as a decimal. Use 🔵1, ⚪0.1 and ⚪0.01 to help you.

(a)   148 hundredths

(b)   213 hundredths

(c) $\dfrac{105}{100}$

(d) $\dfrac{150}{100}$

2 What is the decimal represented by each letter?

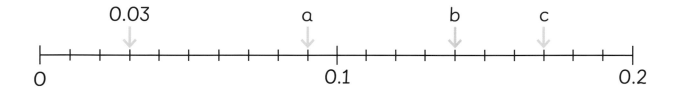

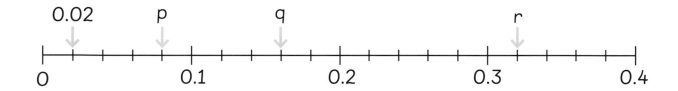

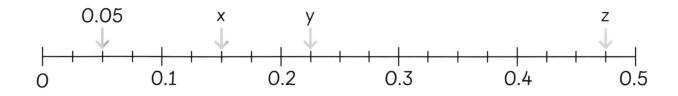

Complete Worksheet **7** – Page **14 – 15** ▶

Writing Decimals

In Focus

What different numbers can you make?

tens	ones	tenths	hundredths

Let's Learn

1 makes

tens	ones	tenths	hundredths
1	3	0	8

The digit 3 stands for 3. **1** **1** **1**

13.08 is read as thirteen and eight hundredths.

2 makes

tens	ones	tenths	hundredths
1	8	3	0

The digit 3 stands for $\frac{3}{10}$. **0.1** **0.1** **0.1**

18.30 is read as eighteen and three tenths.

	tens	ones	tenths	hundredths
makes	0	8	1	3

The digit 3 stands for $\dfrac{3}{100}$.

0.01 0.01 0.01

8.13 is read as eight and thirteen hundredths.

	tens	ones	tenths	hundredths
makes	0	3	1	8

The digit 3 stands for 3.

The digit 1 stands for $\dfrac{1}{10}$.

The digit 8 stands for $\dfrac{8}{100}$.

Guided Practice

What does the digit 6 stand for in each number?

1 2.46 =

2 60.24 =

3 20.46 =

4 26.4 =

5 62.04 =

6 20.64 =

Complete Worksheet **8** – Page **16**

Comparing and Ordering Decimals

In Focus

Roll a dice to make a number.

Place the first digit you roll in the tenths place.

Place the second digit you roll in the hundredths place.

Who makes the smaller number?

Let's Learn

1

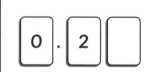

2 tenths is less than 4 tenths.

0.2 is less than 0.4.

0.2 < 0.4

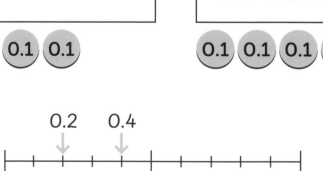

2

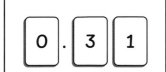

| 0 | . | 3 | 1 |

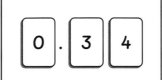

| 0 | . | 3 | 4 |

(0.1) (0.1) (0.1)

(0.01)

(0.1) (0.1) (0.1)

(0.01) (0.01) (0.01) (0.01)

31 hundredths is less than 34 hundredths.

0.31 is less than 0.34.

0.31 < 0.34

```
        0.31         0.34
         ↓            ↓
  |----+----+----+----+----+----+----+----+----|
 0.3                 0.35                  0.4
```

Guided Practice

1 Which number is smaller?

Use to help you.

Write your answers using > or <.

(a) 0.1 or 0.6

(b) 0.03 or 0.02

(c) 0.12 or 0.21

(d) 0.31 or 0.34

2 Which number is greater?

0	0.1	0.2	0.3	0.4	0.5	0.6	0.7	0.8	0.9	1

(a)   0.1 or 0.9

(b)   0.8 or 0.6

Write your answers using > or <.

3 Arrange these numbers in increasing order.

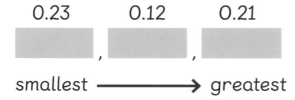

0.23   0.12   0.21

_____ , _____ , _____

smallest ⟶ greatest

4 Arrange these numbers in decreasing order.

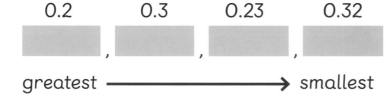

0.2   0.3   0.23   0.32

_____ , _____ , _____ , _____

greatest ⟶ smallest

Complete Worksheet **9** – Page **17 – 18**

Comparing and Ordering Decimals

In Focus

Roll a dice . Place the digit in the ones, tenths or hundredths place. See which player makes the largest number.

Is Emma correct?

> We may know the winner before every player has rolled three times.

Let's Learn

1

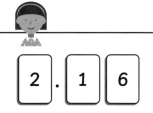
2 . 2 1 and 2 . 1 6

0.1 = 0.01 0.01 0.01 0.01 0.01 0.01 0.01 0.01 0.01 0.01

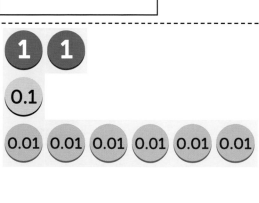

2.21 is greater than 2.16.

2.21 > 2.16

2 Arrange the numbers in increasing order.

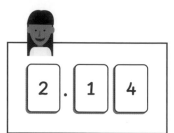

2 . 1 4

| 1 | 1 |
| 0.1 |
| 0.01 | 0.01 | 0.01 | 0.01 |

3 . 1 4

| 1 | 1 |
| 1 |
| 0.1 |
| 0.01 | 0.01 | 0.01 | 0.01 |

2 . 2 2

| 1 | 1 |
| 0.1 |
| 0.1 |
| 0.01 | 0.01 |

3. ▨ ▨ is more than 2. ▨ ▨

2 . 1 4

| 1 | 1 |
| 0.1 |
| 0.01 | 0.01 | 0.01 | 0.01 |

2.1 ▨ is always less than 2.2 ▨ .

2 . 2 2

| 1 | 1 |
| 0.1 |
| 0.1 |
| 0.01 | 0.01 |

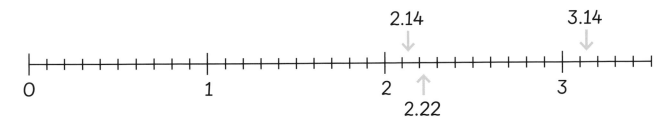

ones		tenths	hundredths
2	•	1	4
2	•	2	2
3	•	1	4

2.14 , 2.22 , 3.14

smallest ⟶ greatest

Guided Practice

1 Which number is smaller?

(a) 3.7 or 7.3

(b) 1.52 or 1.25

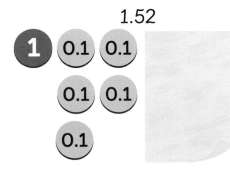

2 Which number is greater?

2.65 or 2.69

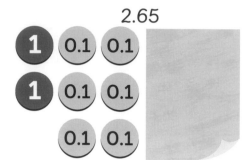

3 Arrange the numbers in increasing order.

(a) 4.51 , 0.12 , 0.21

[   ] , [   ] , [   ]

smallest ——————→ greatest

(b) 2.9 , 8.5 , 3.1

[   ] , [   ] , [   ]

smallest ——————→ greatest

(c) 4.59 , 4.63 , 4.61

[   ] , [   ] , [   ]

smallest ——————→ greatest

Complete Worksheet **10** – Page **19 – 20**

Comparing and Ordering Decimals

In Focus

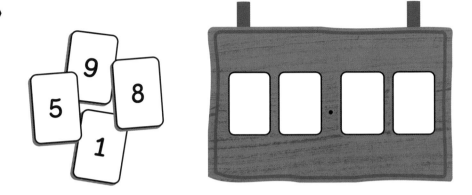

Make four different numbers using $\boxed{5}$, $\boxed{9}$, $\boxed{8}$, $\boxed{1}$ and $\blacksquare$.
Arrange the numbers in order.

Let's Learn

1 makes $\boxed{1}\boxed{5}.\boxed{9}\boxed{8}$, $\boxed{5}\boxed{1}.\boxed{9}\boxed{8}$, $\boxed{8}\boxed{1}.\boxed{9}\boxed{5}$

and $\boxed{9}\boxed{5}.\boxed{1}\boxed{8}$.

smallest ⟶ greatest

2 makes `1` `5` . `8` `9` , `1` `5` . `9` `8` , `5` `1` . `8` `9`

and `5` `1` . `9` `8` .

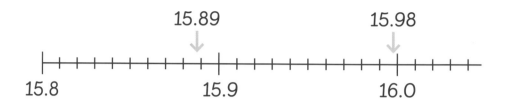

15.89   15.98

15.8   15.9   16.0

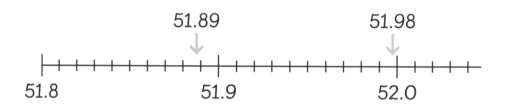

51.89   51.98

51.8   51.9   52.0

tens	ones	tenths	hundredths
1	5	8	9
1	5	9	8
5	1	8	9
5	1	9	8

Guided Practice

1 Which of the following numbers is the smallest?

(a)
| 12.45 | 21.45 | 42.54 | 4.54 |

(b)
| 10.37 | 10.29 | 10.92 | 10.21 |

2 Arrange the numbers in increasing order.

(a)

| 75.42 | 57.42 | 57.24 | 57.48 |

(b)

| 15.09 | 11.12 | 15.11 | 11.08 |

3 Use the digits 0, 3, 5 and 2 to make the greatest possible number.

(a) ☐☐.☐☐

(b) ☐☐☐.☐

Complete Worksheet **11** – Page **21 - 22**

Making Number Patterns

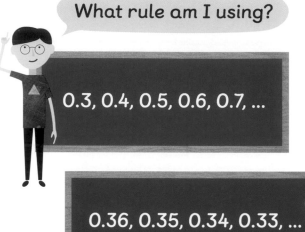

What rule am I using?

0.3, 0.4, 0.5, 0.6, 0.7, ...

What's my rule?

0.36, 0.35, 0.34, 0.33, ...

Can you continue the number patterns?

Let's Learn

1   0.3, 0.4, 0.5, 0.6, 0.7, ...

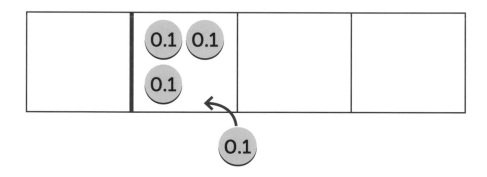

0.4 is 0.1 more than 0.3.

 makes the number pattern by adding 0.1 each time.

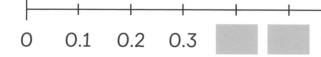

0   0.1   0.2   0.3

2 0.36, 0.35, 0.34, 0.33, ...

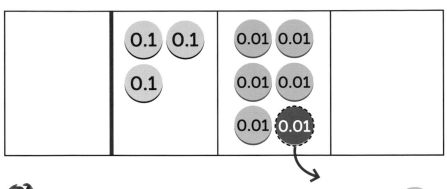

0.35 is 0.01 less than 0.36.

 makes the number pattern by removing 0.01 each time.

0.36 0.37 0.38 0.39 0.4

Can you write down the first six numbers in this number pattern?

Guided Practice

1 What are the next five numbers in each number pattern?

(a) 1.4, 1.5, 1.6, ...

(b) 3.4, 3.3, 3.2, ...

(c) 1.24, 1.25, 1.26, 1.27, 1.28, ...

(d) 5.48, 5.47, 5.46, 5.45, 5.44, ...

Say the numbers out loud.

2 (a) What number is 0.1 more than 4.7?

(b) What number is 0.01 less than 2.42?

3 (a) [ ] is 0.1 less than 5.0.

(b) [ ] is 0.01 more than 5.0.

Complete Worksheet **12** – Page **23 – 24**

Rounding Decimals

In Focus

Draw a line that is 3 cm long.

Let's see whose line is closest to 3 cm long!

Let's Learn

1 draws ——.

0cm 1 2 3 4

 It is 0.9 cm long.

It is about 1 cm long.

0.9 is approximately equal to 1.

0.9 ≈ 1

The sign ≈ means 'approximately equal to'.

2 draws  .

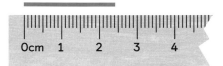

 It is 2.4 cm long.

It is nearer to 2 cm than to 3 cm. It is about 2 cm long.

2.4 is approximately equal to 2.

2.4 ≈ 2

3 draws 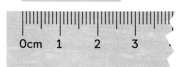 .

 It is 2.6 cm long.

It is nearer to 3 cm than to 2 cm. It is about 3 cm long.

2.6 is approximately equal to 3.

2.6 ≈ 3

4 draws _____ .

It is 3.5 cm long.

It is exactly between 3 cm and 4 cm. We take it to be about 4 cm.

3.5 is approximately equal to 4.

3.5 ≈ 4

Activity Time

Work in groups of 3 or 4.

What you need:

① Measure small objects in your classroom with a .

② Record the reading to 1 decimal place.

③ Round each reading to the nearest centimetre.

Guided Practice

1 Express each measurement as a fraction and as a decimal.

(a)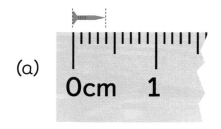

The length of the nail is $\dfrac{4}{10}$ cm or ⬜ cm.

(b)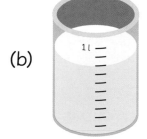

The volume of the water is $\dfrac{\boxed{}}{10}$ l or ⬜ l.

(c)

The total volume of water is $1\dfrac{\boxed{}}{10}$ l or ⬜ l.

(d)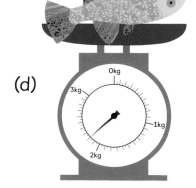

The mass of the fish is $2\dfrac{\boxed{}}{10}$ kg or ⬜ kg.

2 Read each measurement exactly. Record it to the nearest whole number.

(a)

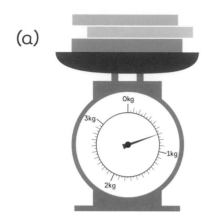

The books weigh 0.7 kg.

0.7 ≈

The mass of the book is about ☐ kg.

(b)

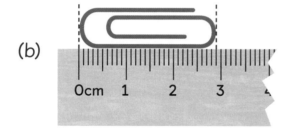

The length of the paper clip is ☐ cm.

☐ ≈

The length of the paper clip is about ☐ cm.

(c)

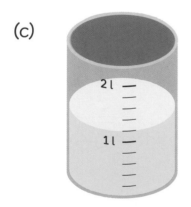

The volume of the water is ☐ l.

☐ ≈

The volume of the water is about ☐ l.

Complete Worksheet **13** – Page **25 – 26**

Rounding Decimals

In Focus

Durian is a popular fruit in Southeast Asia.
The rest of the world hates it.

Estimate the total mass
of these baskets of durians.

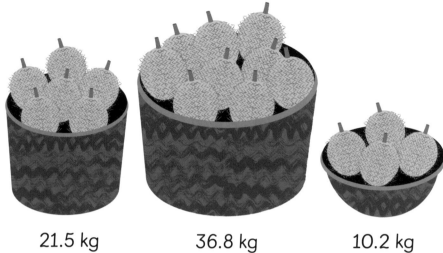

21.5 kg   36.8 kg   10.2 kg

Let's Learn

1 10.2 kg ≈ [   ] kg

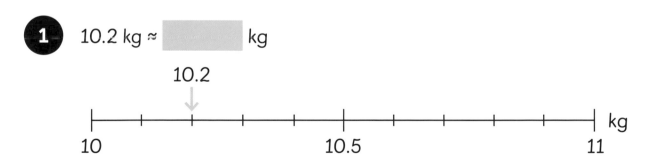

10.2 is nearer to 10 than to 11.

10.2 kg is approximately 10 kg to the nearest kg.

10.2 kg ≈ 10 kg

2   36.8 kg ≈ ⬜ kg

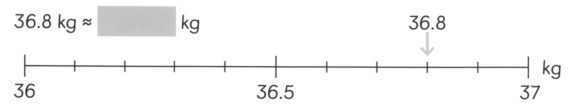

36.8 is nearer to 37 than to 36.

36.8 kg is approximately 37 kg to the nearest kg.

36.8 kg ≈ 37 kg

3   21.5 kg ≈ ⬜ kg

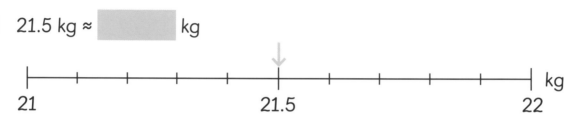

21.5 is exactly in between 21 and 22.

21.5 kg is taken to be approximately

22 kg to the nearest kg.

21.5 kg ≈ 22 kg

> 21.5 kg + 36.8 kg + 10.2 kg
> ≈ 22 kg + 37 kg + 10 kg
> = 69 kg

4   Round 21.5 kg to the nearest 10 kg.

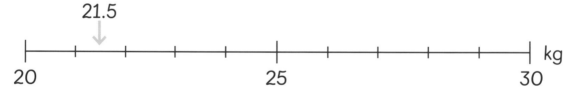

21.5 kg ≈ 20 kg (to the nearest 10 kg)

> 36.8 kg ≈ ⬜
> (to the nearest 10 kg)

> 10.2 kg ≈ ⬜
> (to the nearest 10 kg)

Estimate the total mass of
the three baskets of durians.

> 20 kg + 40 kg + 10 kg

Guided Practice

1 Round each measurement to the nearest mm.

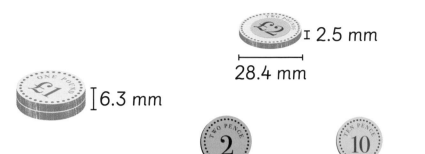

£2 ɪ 2.5 mm

28.4 mm

£1]6.3 mm

20 ɪ 1.7 mm

2 (TWO PENCE)
25.9 mm

10 (TEN PENCE)
24.5 mm

2 Estimate the total mass of these bags by rounding the readings to the nearest kg.

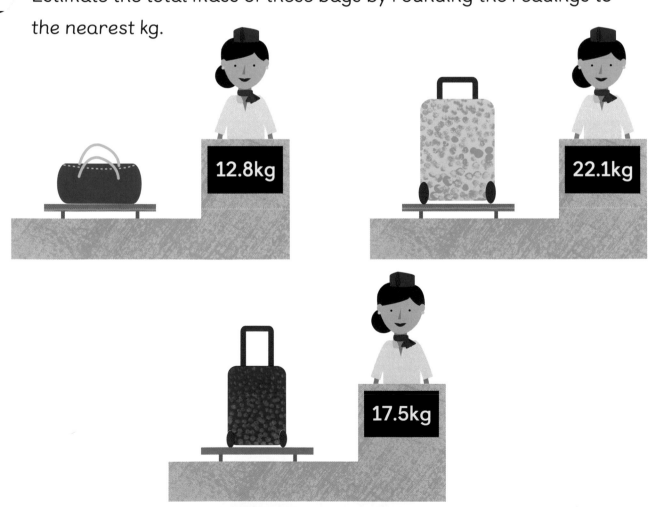

12.8kg

22.1kg

17.5kg

Complete Worksheet 14 – Page 27 - 28

Writing Fractions as Decimals

In Focus

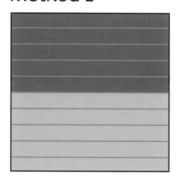

$\frac{1}{2}$ $\frac{1}{4}$ $\frac{3}{4}$

How do we write these fractions as decimals?

Let's Learn

1 $\frac{1}{2}$ =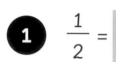

Method 1

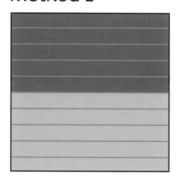

$\frac{1}{2}$ = 5 tenths

= 0.5

Method 2

× 5

$\frac{1}{2} = \dfrac{}{10}$

× 5

$\frac{1}{2} = \dfrac{5}{10}$

= 0.5

2 $\frac{1}{4}$ =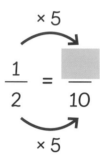

Method 1

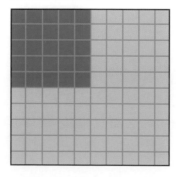

$\frac{1}{4}$ = 25 hundredths

= 0.25

Method 2

× 25

$\frac{1}{4} = \dfrac{}{100}$

× 25

$\frac{1}{4} = \dfrac{25}{100}$

= 0.25

3 $\dfrac{3}{4}$ =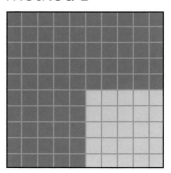

Method 1

$\dfrac{3}{4}$ = 75 hundredths

= 0.75

Method 2

× 25

$\dfrac{3}{4} = \dfrac{}{100}$

× 25

$\dfrac{3}{4} = \dfrac{75}{100}$

= 0.75

4 $\dfrac{1}{2}$ = ⬜ tenths = ⬜ hundredths

      =      =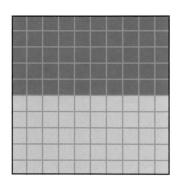

1 half   5 tenths = 0.5   50 hundredths = 0.50

Why not?

It is not necessary to write the zero in the hundredths place.

Guided Practice

1 $\frac{1}{2}$ can be written as tenths.

$$\frac{1}{2} = \frac{\boxed{}}{10} = \boxed{} \text{ tenths}$$

Suggest another fraction that can be written as tenths.

$$\frac{\boxed{}}{\boxed{}} = \frac{\boxed{}}{10} = \boxed{} \text{ tenths}$$

2 $\frac{1}{4}$ and $\frac{3}{4}$ can be written as hundredths.

$$\frac{1}{4} = \frac{25}{100} = \boxed{} \text{ hundredths}$$

$$\frac{3}{4} = \frac{\boxed{}}{100} = \boxed{} \text{ hundredths}$$

Suggest another fraction that can be written as hundredths.

$$\frac{\boxed{}}{\boxed{}} = \frac{\boxed{}}{100} = \boxed{} \text{ hundredths}$$

3 Write each quantity in decimals.

(a) $1\frac{3}{4}$ m

(b) $8\frac{1}{2}$ kg

(c) £ $5\frac{1}{4}$

Suggest something that could have each measurement or value.

Complete Worksheet **15** – Page **29 – 30**

Dividing Whole Numbers by 10

In Focus

10 children share 3 bars of chocolate equally.

What fraction of a chocolate bar does each child get?

1. $3 \div 10 = $ [   ]

$$\frac{1}{10}$$

$$\frac{1}{10}$$

$$\frac{1}{10}$$

Divide each bar into 10 pieces.

Each piece is 1 tenth.

I get 3 tenths.

3 ÷ 10 = 3 tenths
= 0.3

digit 3 in ones place

digit 3 in tenths place

2. What if 10 children share 23 sheets of art paper equally among themselves?

$20 \div 10 = 2$

$\underline{3 \div 10 = 0.3}$

$\overline{23 \div 10 = 2.3}$

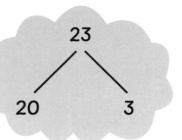

I get 2.3 sheets of paper.

tens	ones	tenths
2	3	

$\div 10$ →

tens	ones	tenths
	2	3

What do you notice when a number is divided by 10?

Guided Practice

Divide by 10.

(a) $8 \div 10 =$ ⬚

8

(b) $42 \div 10 =$ ⬚

42

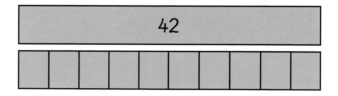

Complete Worksheet **16** – Page **31 - 32**

Dividing Whole Numbers by 100

In Focus

I start with 14 large blocks of soap.

wants to use all the blocks of soap to make 100 packs, all containing the same amount of soap. How much soap is there in each pack?

Let's Learn

1   10 ÷ 100 =

 This bar of soap is 1 tenth of a block.

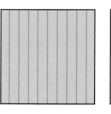  

$$10 \div 100 = 1 \text{ tenth}$$
$$= 0.1$$

digit 1 in
tens place

digit 1 in
tenths place

2   4 ÷ 100 =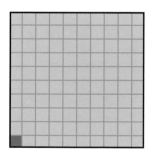

This piece of soap is 1 hundredth of a block of soap.

$$4 \div 100 = 0.04$$

digit 4 in
ones place

digit 4 in
hundredths place

3 $14 \div 100 = \boxed{}$

$$10 \div 100 = 0.1$$
$$\underline{4 \div 100 = 0.04}$$
$$\overline{14 \div 100 = 0.14}$$

tens	ones	tenths	hundredths
1	4 •		

$\div 100$ →

tens	ones	tenths	hundredths
	0 •	1	4

Guided Practice

1 Use a calculator to help you.

Pick any whole number less than 100.

First, divide it by 10.

Then, start again and divide it by 100.

What do you notice about the quotient in each case?

2 Divide.

(a) $7 \div 10$

(b) $7 \div 100$

(c) $59 \div 10$

(d) $59 \div 100$

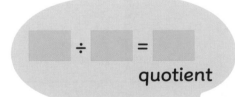

$$\boxed{} \div \boxed{} = \boxed{}$$
quotient

Is it easy to divide whole numbers by 10 or by 100? Why?

Complete Worksheet **17** – Page **33 – 35**

Use a calculator to observe the decimal number we get when 1 is divided by another whole number.

$1 \div 2$ =
$1 \div 3$ =
$1 \div 4$ =
$1 \div 5$ =
$1 \div 6$ =
$1 \div 7$ =

$1 \div 8$ =
$1 \div 9$ =
$1 \div 10$ =
$1 \div 11$ =
$1 \div 12$ =

Is it possible to tell the digit in the 10th decimal place in each case?

1st
↓
$1 \div 7 = 0.142 \ 857 \ 14$
↑
8th

Simon Stevin introduced decimals in the late 16th century. His notation was more cumbersome: he did not use a decimal point, but wrote 3.14 as:

3 (0) 1 (1) 4

Why do you think Stevin invented decimals?

Find some examples of decimals used in everyday situations.

Why do people 'invent' decimals?

Self Check

I know how to...

- ☐ recognise and write tenths.

- ☐ recognise and write hundredths.

- ☐ compare numbers with the same number of decimal places.

- ☐ complete number patterns involving decimals.

- ☐ round decimals with one decimal place to the nearest whole number.

- ☐ recognise and write decimal equivalents of $\frac{1}{4}$, $\frac{1}{2}$ and $\frac{3}{4}$.

- ☐ divide a 1- or 2-digit number by 10.

- ☐ divide a 1- or 2-digit number by 100.

- ☐ solve simple measure and money problems involving decimals.

Chapter 9
Money

Writing Amounts of Money

In Focus

Is this enough for me to pay for a smoothie?

£1.30 per bottle

smoothie
250ml

Let's Learn

1 10p = £ ⬜

£ $\frac{1}{10}$

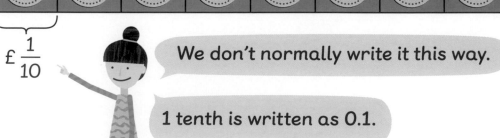

We don't normally write it this way.

1 tenth is written as 0.1.

10p = £0.10

2 Write the amount in £.

£ $\frac{1}{2}$

We write 5 tenths of a pound as £0.50.

We write as £1.50.

3 Show £1.30.

£1.30

£1   £0.30

£ $\frac{3}{10}$

This is 30p.

this is £1.30

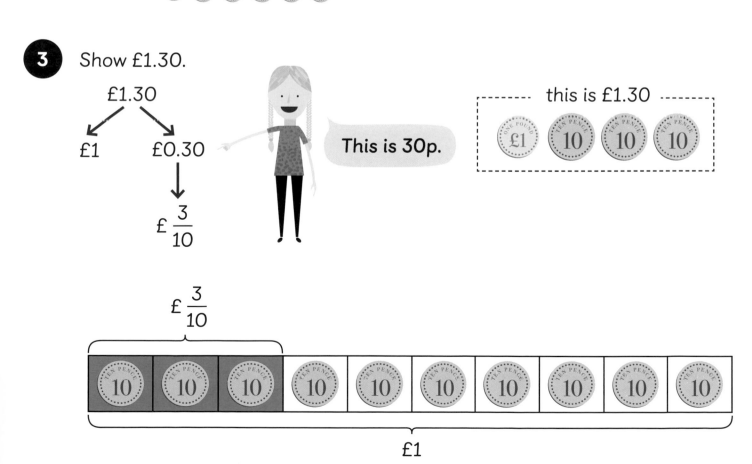

£ $\frac{3}{10}$

£1

1

£1

Write the amount of money in £.

(a)   £ [   ]

(b)   £ [   ]

(c)   £ [   ]

2 Match the amounts that are equal.

Sweets
£1.20

Hazelnuts
£2.10

£1.90

Biscuits

•   •   •

•   •   •

| £2 and 10p | £1 and 90p | £1 and 20p |

Complete Worksheet **1** – Page **43 – 44**

Writing Amounts of Money

In Focus

Who has written the amount correctly?

£0.50   £5.00   £0.05

Let's Learn

1   1p = £ [   ]

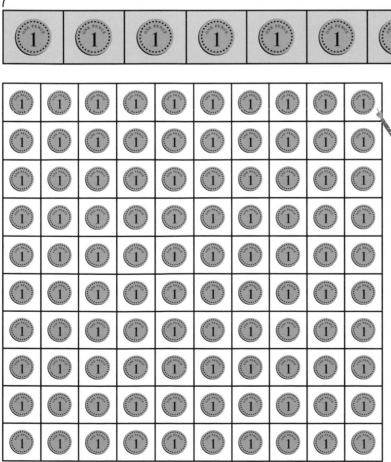

1p is $\frac{1}{100}$ of £1.

1p = £0.01

2 5p = £ [____]

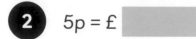 £0.01

10p = £0.10

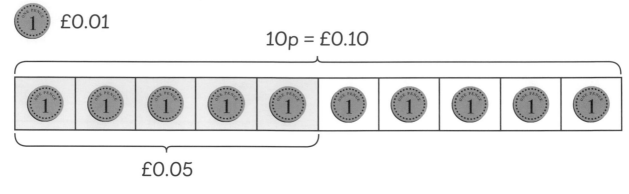

£0.05

5p = £0.05

3 £0.50 = [____] p

£1

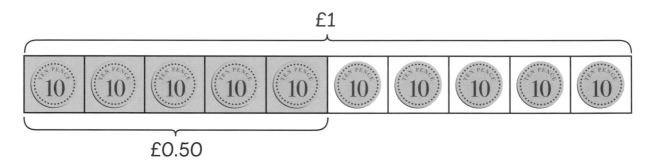

£0.50

4 Write the amount shown in £.

£0.20   £0.10   £0.05   £0.01

£2 and 36p = £2.36

1 Write the amount of money in £.

(a)  £ ____

(b) £ ____

(c) £ ____

2 Match the amounts that are equal.

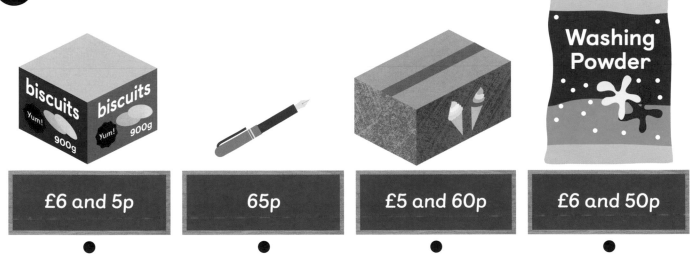

| £6 and 5p | 65p | £5 and 60p | £6 and 50p |
| • | • | • | • |

£6.50   £6.05   £5.60   £5.06   £0.65

Complete Worksheet 2 – Page 45 – 46 ▶

Comparing Amounts of Money

In Focus

Compare the prices of different fruit.

Let's Learn

1

£3 is already more than £2.30.

£3. ▨▨ is always more than £2. ▨▨.

£3.20 is more than £2.30.

2

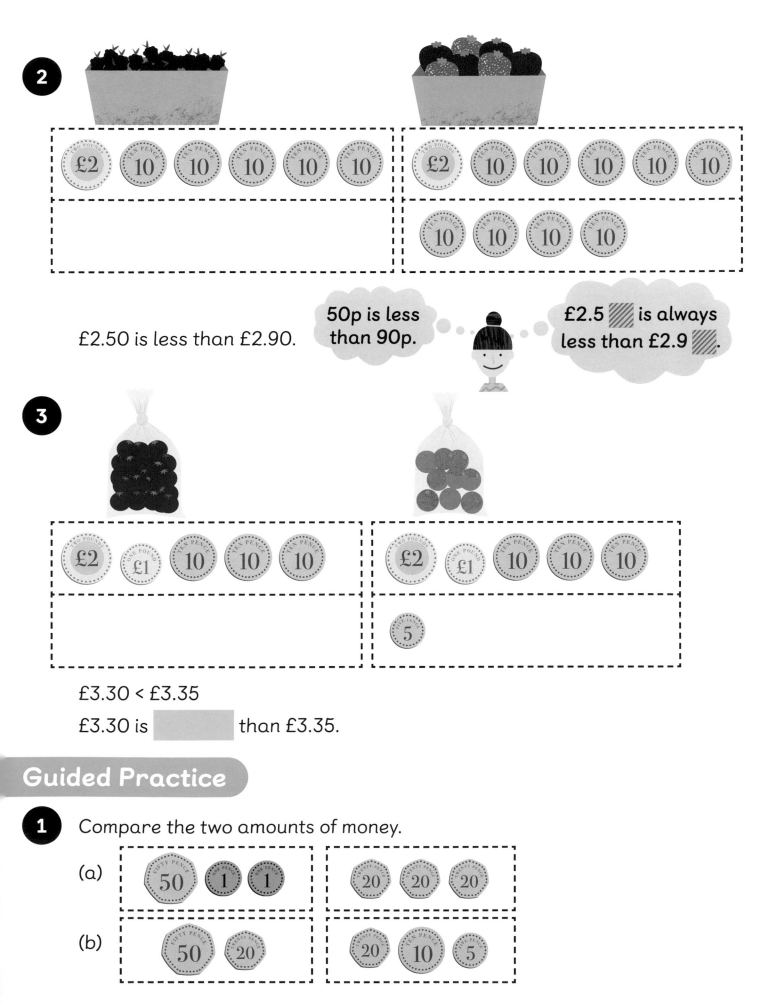

£2.50 is less than £2.90.

50p is less than 90p.

£2.5 ▨ is always less than £2.9 ▨.

3

£3.30 < £3.35

£3.30 is ▨ than £3.35.

1 Compare the two amounts of money.

(a)

(b)

(c)

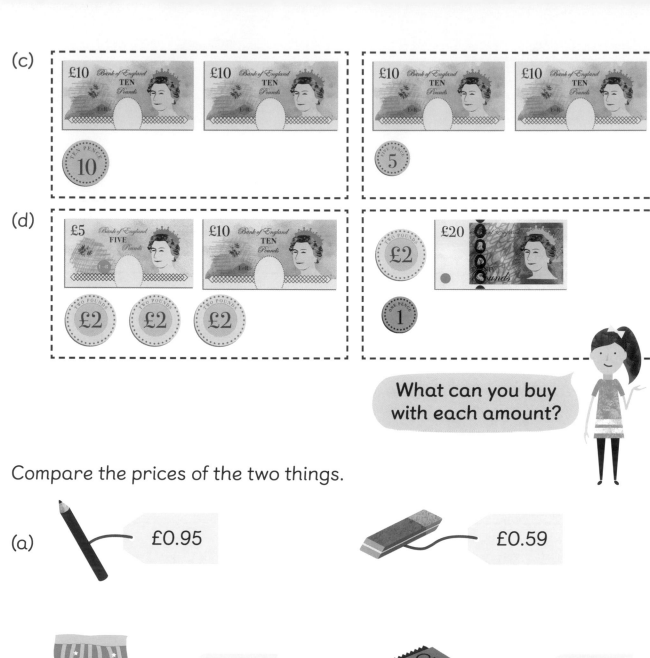

(d)

What can you buy
with each amount?

2 Compare the prices of the two things.

(a)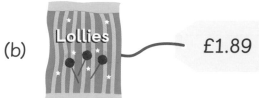
£0.95

£0.59

(b) £1.89

£1.85

(c)
£2.50

£2.05

Complete Worksheet 3 – Page 47

Rounding Amounts of Money

In Focus

£2.50 per item

£2.10 per cup

£1.80 per item

I bought something that is about £2.

What did 😊 buy?

Let's Learn

1 Round £2.10 to the nearest £.

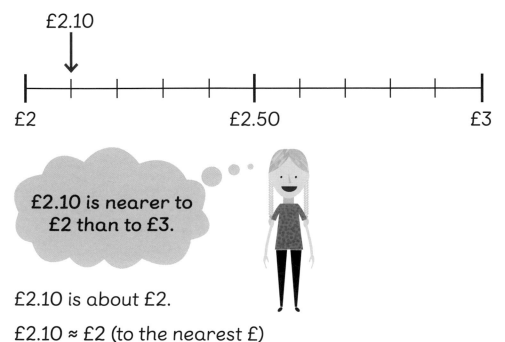

£2.10

£2   £2.50   £3

£2.10 is nearer to £2 than to £3.

£2.10 is about £2.

£2.10 ≈ £2 (to the nearest £)

2 Round £1.80 to the nearest £.

£1.80 is nearer to £2 than to £1.

£1.80 is about £2.

£1.80 ≈ £2 (to the nearest £)

3 Round £2.50 to the nearest £.

£2.50 ≈ £

£2.50 is exactly in between £2 and £3.

We take £2.50 to be approximately £3.

£2.50 ≈ £3 (to the nearest £)

1 Round each amount to the nearest £.

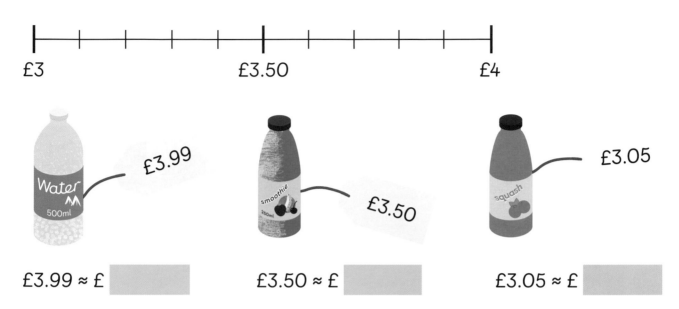

£3.99 ≈ £ [ ]   £3.50 ≈ £ [ ]   £3.05 ≈ £ [ ]

2 Round each amount to the nearest £ and to the nearest £10.

(a)

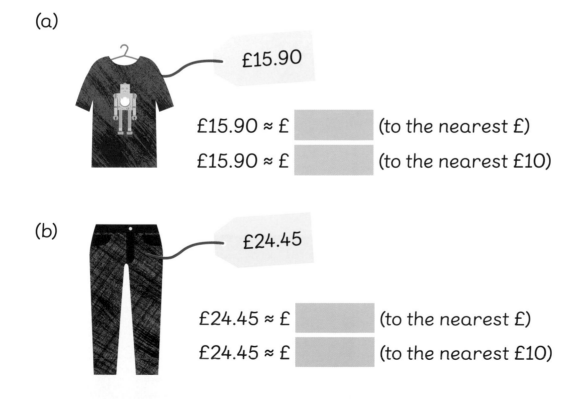

£15.90 ≈ £ [ ]   (to the nearest £)
£15.90 ≈ £ [ ]   (to the nearest £10)

(b)

£24.45 ≈ £ [ ]   (to the nearest £)
£24.45 ≈ £ [ ]   (to the nearest £10)

Complete Worksheet **4 – Page 48 – 49**

Solving Problems Involving Money

In Focus

 wants to buy these.

 £2.63

£1.26

£2.80

Is this enough to pay for them?

Let's Learn

 1

£2.63

£1.26

£2.63 → £2 63p

£1.26 → £1 26p

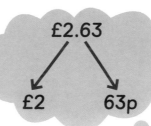

 £2

 50

 10

 1

 1

 1

 £1

 20

 5

 1

£2 + £1 = £3

```
   6  3
+  2  6
-------
   8  9
```

63p + 26p = 89p

Together they cost £3 and 89p or £3.89.

2 £3.89 + £2.80 = £ [____]

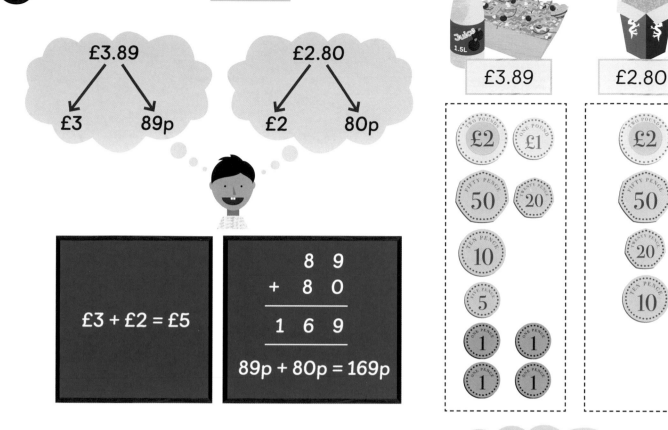

£3.89 → £3, 89p

£2.80 → £2, 80p

£3 + £2 = £5

$$\begin{array}{r} 8\ 9 \\ +\ 8\ 0 \\ \hline 1\ 6\ 9 \end{array}$$

89p + 80p = 169p

£3.89

£2.80

Altogether they cost £6 and 69p or £6.69.

169p = £1 and 69p = £1.69

3 Calculate the change.

£7 – £6.69 = £ [____]

£7 → £6, £1 = 100p

£6 – £6 = £0

100p – 69p = 31p

The change is 31p.

Lemon tart
sit down: £2.10
takeaway: £1.80

Granola bar
sit down: £1.95
takeaway: £1.65

Coffee
sit down: £2.65
takeaway: £2.40

1 Calculate the total each person has to pay.

(a)

sit down

(b)

takeaway

2 Calculate the change.

(a)

takeaway

(b)

sit down

3 Is there enough money to buy these?

(a)

sit down

(b)

takeaway

Complete Worksheet **5** – Page **50 – 51**

Solving Problems Involving Money

In Focus

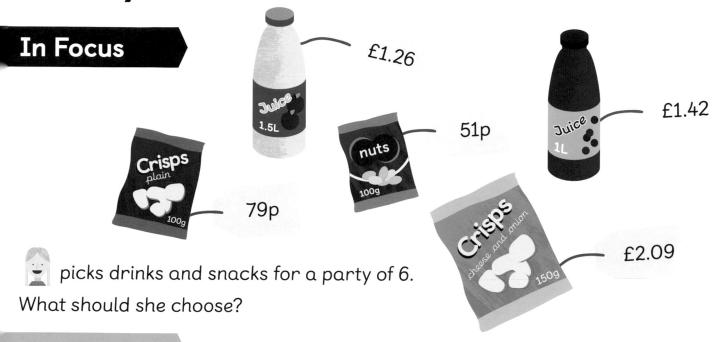

£1.26

£1.42

51p

79p

£2.09

 picks drinks and snacks for a party of 6.
What should she choose?

Let's Learn

1 buys  .

£1.26 × 3 = £ ▢

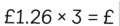

£1.26

£1   26p

£1 × 3 = £3

This is easy.

£3 and 78p

£1.26 × 3 = £3.78

26p × 3 = ▢ p

```
    2  6
  ×    3
  -------
    7  8
```

26p × 3 = 78p

 pays £3.78 for the drinks.

2 buys  and .

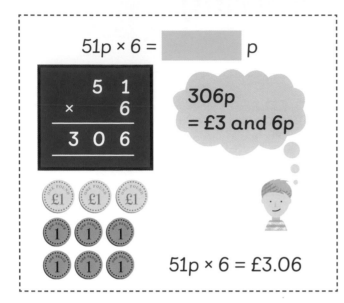

$51p \times 6 =$ ⬚ p

$306p$
$= £3$ and $6p$

$51p \times 6 = £3.06$

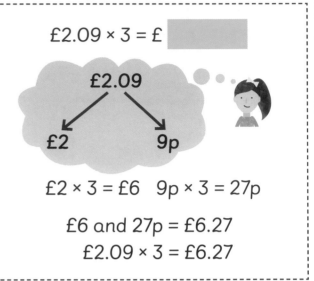

$£2.09 \times 3 = £$ ⬚

$£2.09$

$£2$ $9p$

$£2 \times 3 = £6$ $9p \times 3 = 27p$

$£6$ and $27p = £6.27$
$£2.09 \times 3 = £6.27$

Alternatively,

$50p \times 6$

$1p \times 6$

50 and 50 is £1.

She pays £3.06 for the nuts.

She pays £6.27 for the crisps.

3 $£3.06 + £6.27 = £$ ⬚

£3 and 6p

£6 and 27p

$£3 + £6 = £9$ $6p + 27p = 33p$

 pays £9 and 33p or £9.33 for the snacks.

Can you calculate how much the drinks and snacks cost 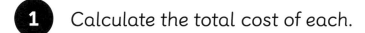 ?

Is £15 enough?

Guided Practice

1 Calculate the total cost of each.

(a)   £1.42 × 2 = £ ⬚

(b)   £1.26 × 5 = £ ⬚

(c)   79p × 4 = ⬚ p

(d)

£1.26 × 3 = £ ⬚

£1.42 × 3 = £ ⬚

£ ⬚ + £ ⬚ = £ ⬚

2 Calculate the change.

Complete Worksheet **6** – Page **52 - 53**

Solving Problems Involving Money

In Focus

 and share the cost of a gift for a friend.

How much does each of them pay?

Let's Learn

1   What if they share the cost equally?

£16.20

£16.20 ÷ 2 = £

£16 ÷ 2 = £8
20p ÷ 2 = 10p

 pays £8 and 10p or £8.10. So does .

£16.20

£16   20p

2 What if pays twice as much as  ?

 ?

} £16.20

£16.20 ÷ 3 = £ [ ]

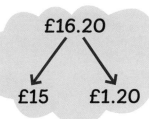

£16.20

£15   £1.20

£15 ÷ 3 = £5

£1.20 = 120p

120p ÷ 3 = 40p

 pays £5 and 40p or £5.40.

 pays £ [ ] .

3 What if 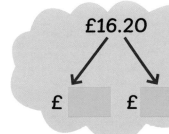 pays 4 times as much as ?

?

} £16.20

£16.20

£ [ ]   £ [ ]

£16.20 ÷ [ ] = £ [ ]

1   and share the cost of a present.

£12

(a) What if they share the cost equally?

(b) What if 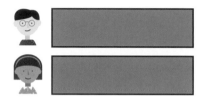 pays twice as much as ?

(c) What if pays three times as much as ?

What if £13.20 ?

2 The total amount in both containers is £1.20.

£1.20 is £1 and 20p.

Suggest the amounts in each container if:

(a) contains twice as much money as 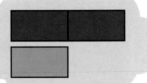 .

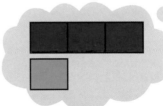

(b) contains three times as much money as .

(c)  contains $\frac{1}{4}$ as much money as .

Complete Worksheet **7** – Page **54 - 55**

Estimating Amounts of Money

In Focus

Estimate the total amount paid for dinner at a restaurant.

Round each item to the nearest pound.

Does 's method give an answer that is more or less than the actual total?

Thai House

VAT 929208510
52 - 54 Faulkner St
Manchester UK M1
(161) 228-1822

Server : Bonny
Dine in
Table : 54
Number of guests : 4

Fish cakes	£6.90
Meat toasties	£5.40
Green curry	£8.90
Mango seabass	£16.90
King prawn curry	£13.90
Chicken salad	£7.50
3 rice	£6.00
4 smoothies	£15.80

Total Amount

For 6 people or more, a 10% service charge will apply. Thank you.

Let's Learn

1 Which amount is rounded down?

Fish cakes	£6.90
Meat toasties	£5.40
Green curry	£8.90
Mango seabass	£16.90
King prawn curry	£13.90
Chicken salad	£7.50
3 rice	£6.00
4 smoothies	£15.80

An example of rounding down is £1.05 ≈ £1.

An example of rounding up is £1.95 ≈ £2.

£5.40
↓

£5   £5.50   £6

£5.40 ≈ £5

2 Which amounts are rounded up?

Fish cakes	£6.90
Meat toasties	£5.40
Green curry	£8.90
Mango seabass	£16.90
King prawn curry	£13.90
Chicken salad	£7.50
3 rice	£6.00
4 smoothies	£15.80

£7
£9
£17
£14
£16

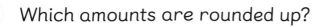

Fish cakes	£6.90
Meat toasties	£5.40
Green curry	£8.90
Mango seabass	£16.90
King prawn curry	£13.90
Chicken salad	£7.50
3 rice	£6.00
4 smoothies	£15.80

£8

Estimate the total amount.

Fish cakes	£6.90	£7
Meat toasties	£5.40	£5
Green curry	£8.90	£9
Mango seabass	£16.90	£17
King prawn curry	£13.90	£14
Chicken salad	£7.50	£8
3 rice	£6.00	£6
4 smoothies	£15.80	£16

There is no need to estimate this.

Estimate the price of 1 smoothie.

£15.80 ≈ £16

£15.80 ÷ 4 ≈ £

Work in groups of 3 or 4.

(1) Make up or collect a receipt for about 6 items.

(2) Estimate the total amount.

(3) Ask your friends to do the same.

(4) Does everyone get the same estimate? Why or why not?

(5) Repeat (2) to (4) using receipts your friends made or brought.

What you need:

Finelli's

Total £1146

Guided Practice

Estimate the total amount of these items by rounding the prices to the nearest £.

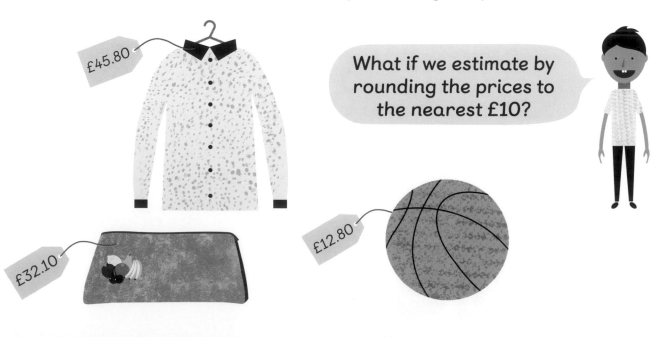

£45.80

£32.10

£12.80

What if we estimate by rounding the prices to the nearest £10?

Complete Worksheet **8** – Page **56 – 57**

Treats
£1.55 for 1
Any 2 for £2.50
Any 3 for £3.25

I bought some treats for a party. I paid £43.80.

£43.80 is £43 and 80p.

How many treats did buy?

Look at the prices of things at the market or at the grocer. Make a list of about five of your favourite foods. Write story problems based on the list.

Solve the problems.

You may solve the problems your friends wrote instead.

Make your stories interesting.

Self Check

I know how to...

☐ count an amount of money and write it using decimals.

☐ compare different amounts of money.

☐ round money to the nearest £ and to the nearest £10.

☐ estimate total amounts of money.

☐ solve problems involving money.

What are some measurements you can see?

Chapter 10
Mass, Volume and Length

Measuring Mass

In Focus

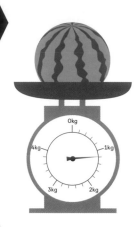

The mass of 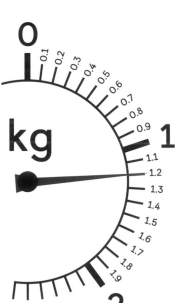 is about 1 kg 200 g.

How heavy is it in kg?

Let's Learn

1 What is the mass of 🍉 ?

1 kg = 1000 g

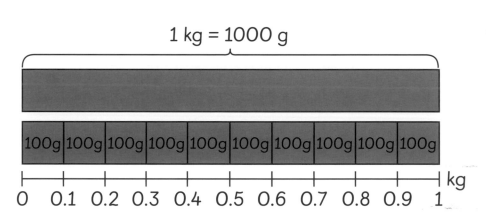

| 100g | 100g | 100g | 100g | 100g | 100g | 100g | 100g | 100g | 100g |

kg

0   0.1   0.2   0.3   0.4   0.5   0.6   0.7   0.8   0.9   1

The mass of the watermelon is about 1.2 kg.

2 Estimate the mass of 🍉 to the nearest kg.

1.2 kg

1 kg   2 kg

1.2 kg is nearer to 1 kg than to 2 kg.

1.2 kg ≈ 1 kg (to the nearest kg)

Guided Practice

What is the mass of each item?

(a)

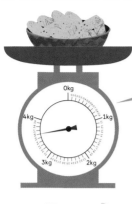

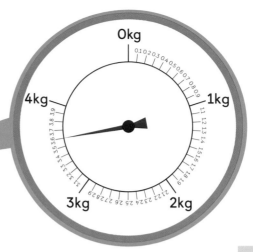

The mass of the basket of potatoes is about [   ] kg.

(b)

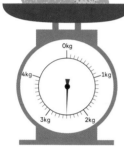

Give the mass of the chicken to the nearest 0.1 kg.

What is its mass to the nearest kg? [   ] kg

(c)

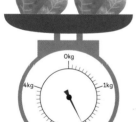

Give the mass of the cabbages to the nearest 0.1 kg.

What is their mass to the nearest kg? [   ] kg

(d)

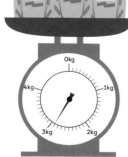

Give the mass of the bags of flour to the nearest 0.1 kg.

What is their mass to the nearest kg? [   ] kg

Complete Worksheet **1** – Page **65 – 66**

Measuring Mass

In Focus

Pick two bags of rice that weigh the same.

Who is correct?

Let's Learn

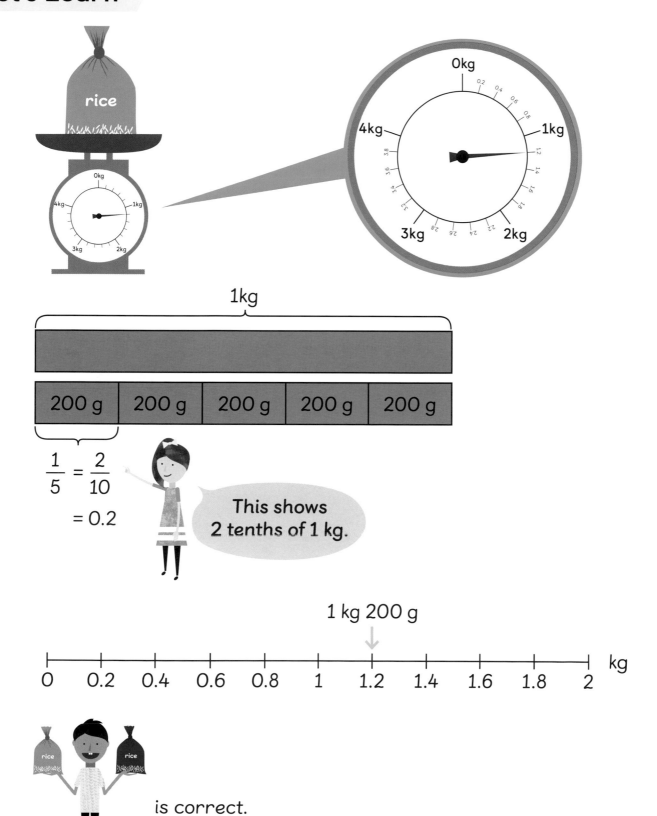

$$\frac{1}{5} = \frac{2}{10}$$
$$= 0.2$$

This shows 2 tenths of 1 kg.

1 kg 200 g

is correct.

Guided Practice

What is the mass of each item?

(a)

The bag of apples weighs about ☐ kg.

(b)

The bag of rice weighs about ☐ kg.

(c)

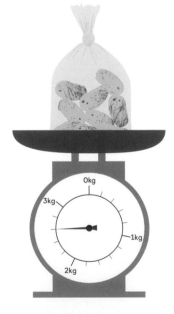

The mass of the bag of potatoes is about ☐ kg.

(d)

The mass of the bag of sugar is about ☐ kg.

Complete Worksheet 2 – Page 67 – 68

Converting Units of Mass

In Focus

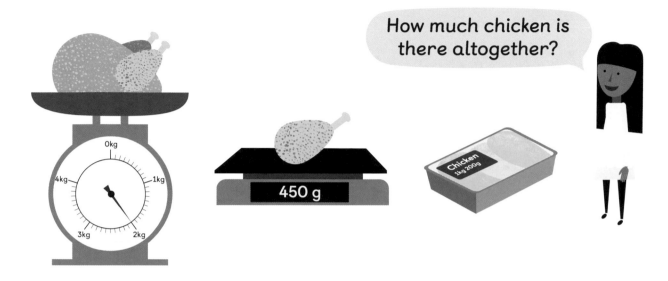

How much chicken is there altogether?

450 g

Chicken 1kg 200g

About 3.5 kg of chicken is needed to cook a curry for a party of about 20 people. Is there enough chicken here?

Let's Learn

1   2 kg = ▢ g

1 kg = 1000 g

1 kg	1 kg
1000 g	1000 g

2 1 kg 200 g = [   ] g

1 kg

1000 g

1000 g + 200 g = 1200 g

3 2 kg + 1 kg 200 g + 450 g = [   ] g

2000 g + 1200 g + 450 g

= [   ] g

4 3.5 kg = [   ] g

3.5 kg is $3\frac{1}{2}$ kg.

1 kg	1 kg	1 kg	$\frac{1}{2}$ kg	

1000 g	1000 g	1000 g	500 g

Is there enough chicken to cook a curry for the group?

Guided Practice

1 What is the mass of each item in g?

(a)
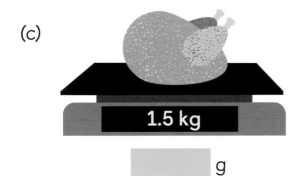

2 kg 250 g

[   ] g

(b)

3 kg

[   ] g

(c)

1.5 kg

[   ] g

2 Which parcel is heavier?

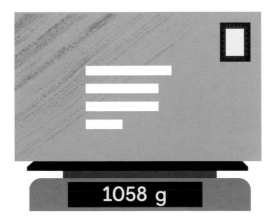

1 kg 580 g

1058 g

Complete Worksheet **3** – Page **69 - 70**

Measuring Volume

In Focus

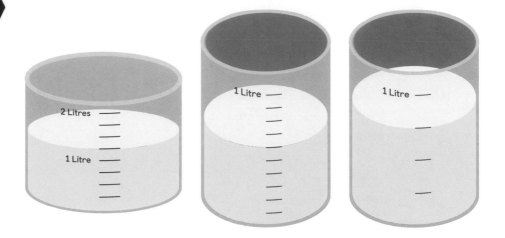

Which container has the greatest amount of water?

Which container has the least amount of water?

Let's Learn

1 Volume of water = ⬜ l

It's less than 1l...

but more than $\frac{1}{2}$ l.

1 tenth

| 0.1 |
| 0.1 |
| 0.1 |
| 0.1 |
| 0.1 |
| 0.1 |
| 0.1 |
| 0.1 |
| 0.1 |
| 0.1 |

1

1 Litre
0.9
0.8
0.7
0.6
0.5
0.4
0.3
0.2
0.1

2   Volume of water = [   ] l

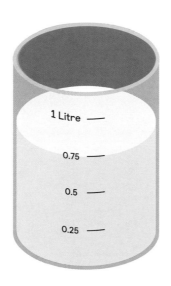

25 hundredths

1

0.25
0.25
0.25
0.25

1 Litre ——
0.75 ——
0.5 ——
0.25 ——

It's less than 1l...

$$\frac{3}{4} = \frac{75}{100}$$

3   Volume of water = [   ] l

25 hundredths

1

0.25
0.25
0.25
0.25

2 litres ——
——
——
1 Litre ——
——
——
——

Guided Practice

1 The drink in each container is poured into a measuring cylinder. Match.

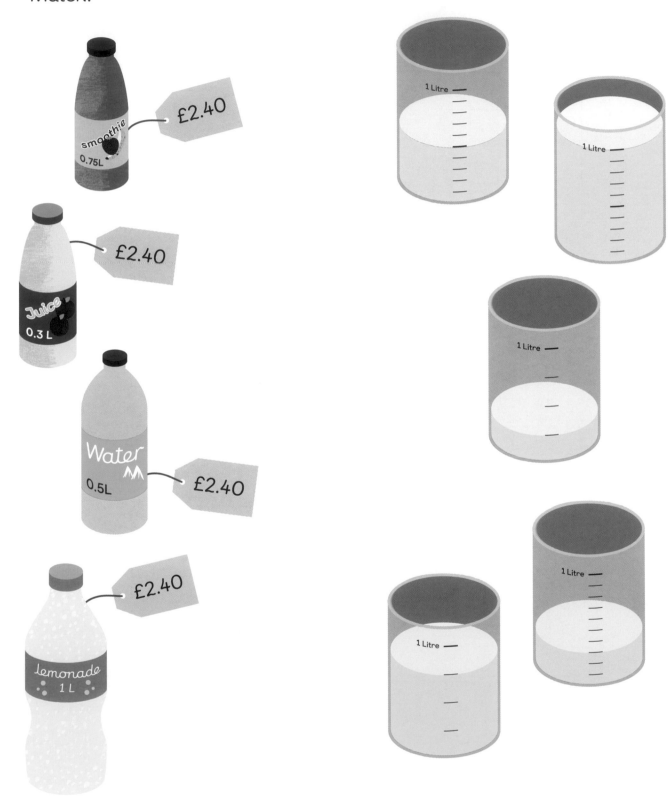

2 The contents from each item are poured into

1 Litre ——

For each item, indicate the position of the liquid in the container.

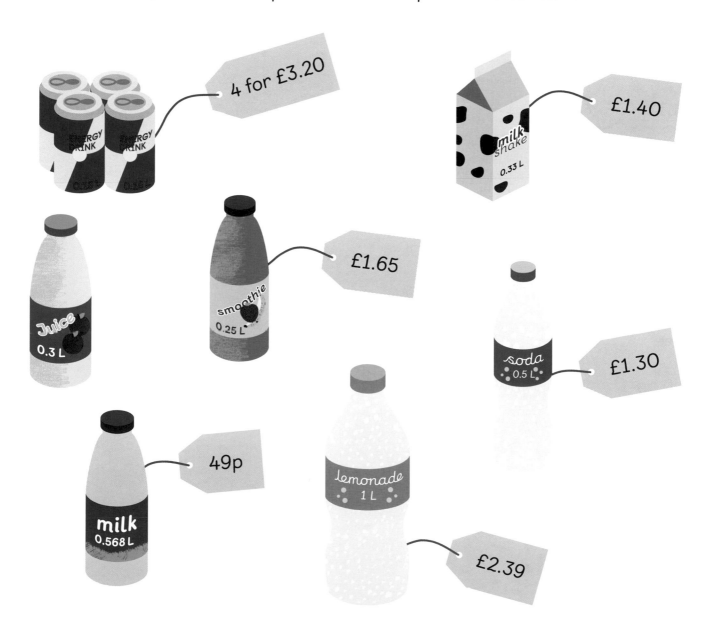

4 for £3.20

£1.40

£1.65

£1.30

49p

£2.39

Complete Worksheet 4 – Page 71 - 72

Measuring Volume

In Focus

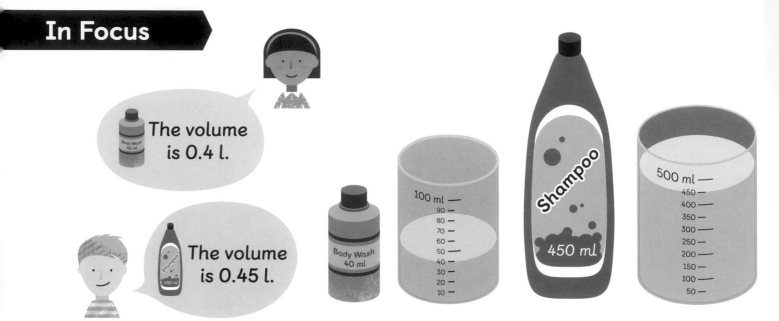

Who is correct?

Let's Learn

1 Volume of the body wash = ⬚ l

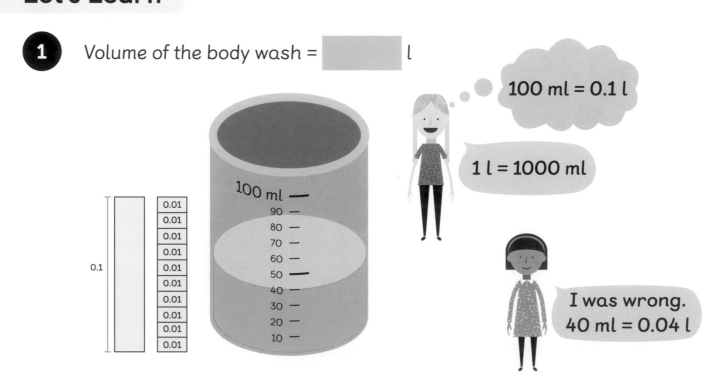

100 ml = 0.1 l

1 l = 1000 ml

I was wrong.
40 ml = 0.04 l

2 Volume of the shampoo = l

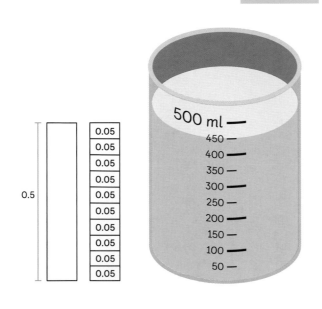

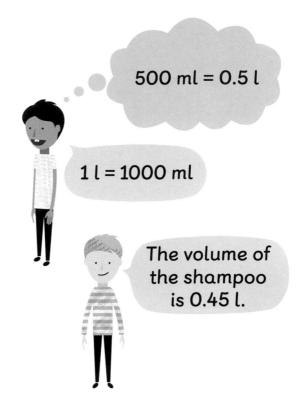

500 ml = 0.5 l

1 l = 1000 ml

The volume of the shampoo is 0.45 l.

Guided Practice

1 These beakers contain coloured water.
What is the volume of water in each beaker?

(a)

The volume of coloured water in the beaker is about [   ] l

(b)

The volume of coloured water in the beaker is about [   ] l

(c)

The volume of coloured water in the beaker is about [   ] l

2 Find the volume of coloured water in each beaker.

(a)

Volume of coloured water = [   ] l

(b)

Volume of coloured water = [   ] l

(c)

Volume of coloured water = [   ] l

Complete Worksheet **5** – Page **73 – 74**

Converting Units of Volume

In Focus

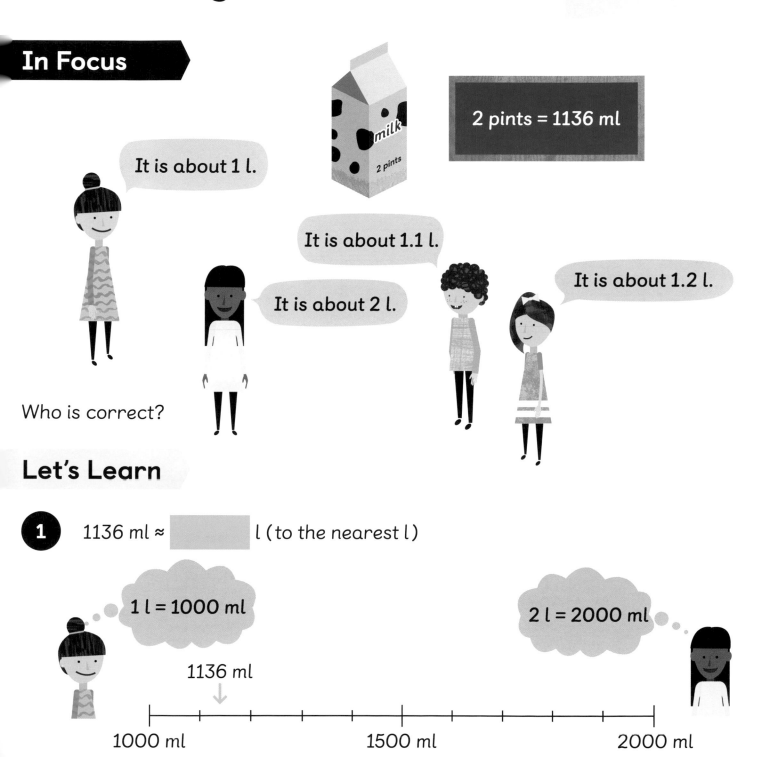

2 pints = 1136 ml

It is about 1 l.

It is about 1.1 l.

It is about 2 l.

It is about 1.2 l.

Who is correct?

Let's Learn

1. 1136 ml ≈ [____] l (to the nearest l)

1 l = 1000 ml

2 l = 2000 ml

1136 ml

1000 ml   1500 ml   2000 ml

1136 ml is closer to 1000 ml than to 2000 ml.

1136 ml ≈ 1000 ml (to the nearest 1000 ml)

 We can also say
1136 ml ≈ 1 l (to the nearest litre).

 It is about 1 l.

is more accurate than   It is about 2 l.

2   1136 ml ≈ ⬚ l (to the nearest 100 ml)

1 l

1

1000 ml

1.1 l = 1100 ml

100 ml

| 0.1 | 0.1 | 0.1 | 0.1 | 0.1 | 0.1 | 0.1 | 0.1 | 0.1 | 0.1 |

0.1 l

 1.1 l = 1100 ml

1.2 l = 1200 ml

1136 ml

1100 ml   1150 ml   1200 ml

1136 ml is closer to 1100 ml than to 1200 ml

1136 ml ≈ 1100 ml (to the nearest 100 ml)

Who is more accurate?

 It is about 1.1 l.   or   It is about 1.2 l.

3 1136 ml ≈ [   ] l (to the nearest 500 ml)

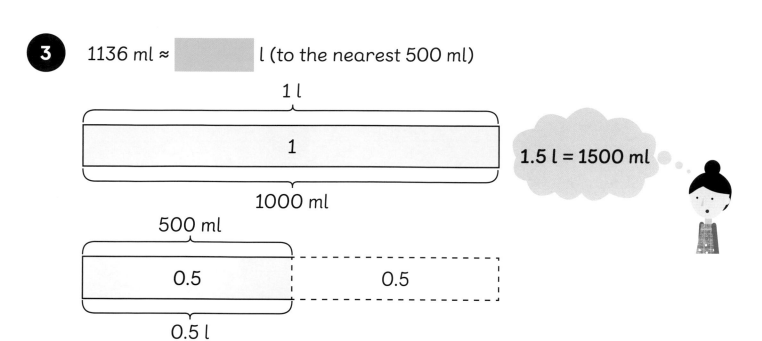

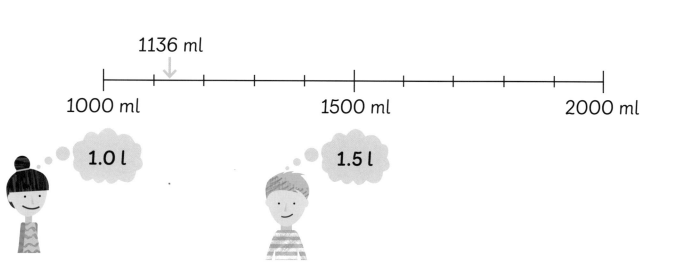

Is 1136 ml closer to 1000 ml or to 1500 ml?

1136 ml ≈ [   ] l (to the nearest 0.5 l)

Guided Practice

1 What is the volume of each bottle of smoothie in ml?

(a)

(b)

smoothie 0.5 l

smoothie 1.8 L

[____] ml

[____] ml

2

ACID

ACID

One bottle holds 1.3 l of acid. The other bottle holds 1 l 30 ml of acid.

Is it possible to tell which bottle is which?

Complete Worksheet 6 – Page 75 – 76

Measuring Height

In Focus

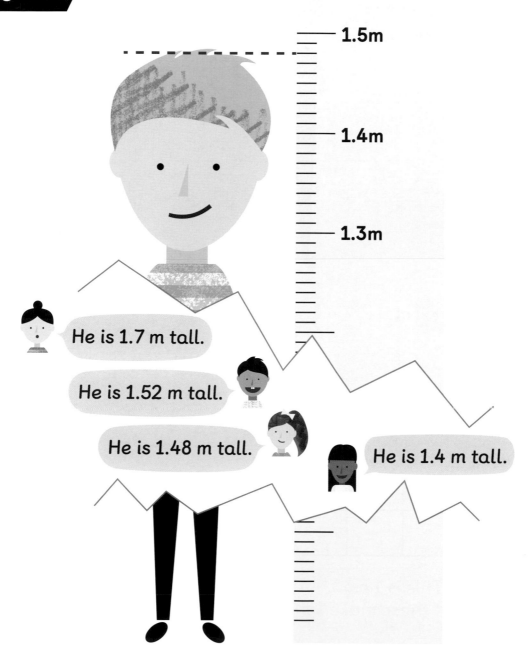

Explain how each child arrives at his or her conclusion.

Who is correct?

Let's Learn

1   10 cm = [____] m

This is 10 cm. Ten of these make 1 m.

This is $\frac{1}{10}$ m or 0.1 m.

1.5m
1.4m
1.3m

2   1 cm = [____] m

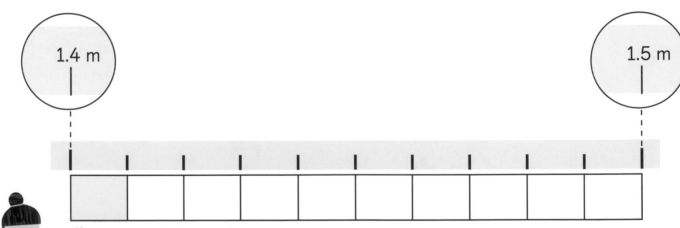

1.4 m

1.5 m

This is 1 cm. 100 of these make 1 m.

This is $\frac{1}{100}$ m or 0.01 m.

3 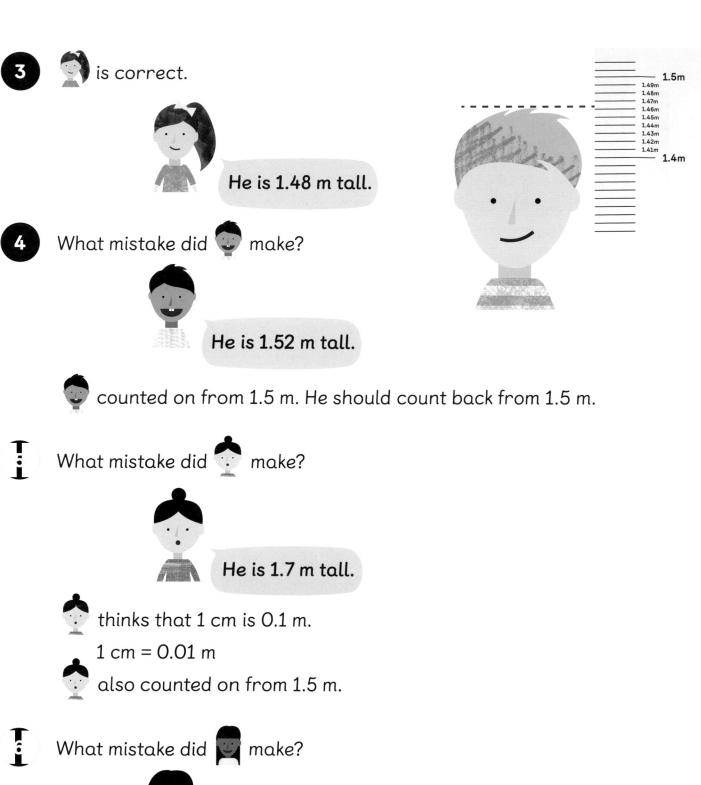 is correct.

He is 1.48 m tall.

4 What mistake did make?

He is 1.52 m tall.

counted on from 1.5 m. He should count back from 1.5 m.

What mistake did make?

He is 1.7 m tall.

thinks that 1 cm is 0.1 m.

1 cm = 0.01 m

also counted on from 1.5 m.

What mistake did make?

He is 1.45 m tall.

 thinks that any height between 1.4 m and 1.5 m is 1.45 m.

She is mistaken.

Work in groups of 4.

① Take turns to measure the height of each person in the group.

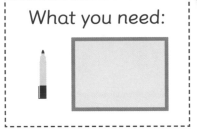

② Record the name and the height of each person. Write the height in metres as a decimal and as a mixed number.

Name	Height as a decimal	Height as a mixed number
Sam	1.34 m	$1\frac{34}{100}$ m

You can also try out this activity by measuring and recording the weight of the people in your group.

Guided Practice

How tall is each person?

(a)

1.2 m 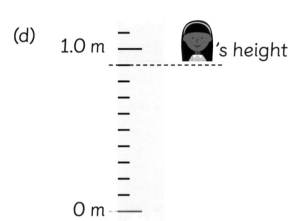's height

1.1 m

(b)

1.7 m

's height

1.6 m

(c)

1.4 m

's height

1.3 m

(d)

1.0 m 's height

0 m

(e)

1 m 's height

0 m

Complete Worksheet **7** – Page **77 – 78**

Measuring Length

In Focus

perimeter

Is the perimeter of the triangle more than 20 cm?

This is 10 cm.

Let's Learn

1. Length of RY = ⬚ cm

We use letters to name vertices and pairs of letters to name the sides.

T

Y

R

10 cm

10.7 cm

2 Length of TR = [   ] cm

Length of TY = [   ] cm

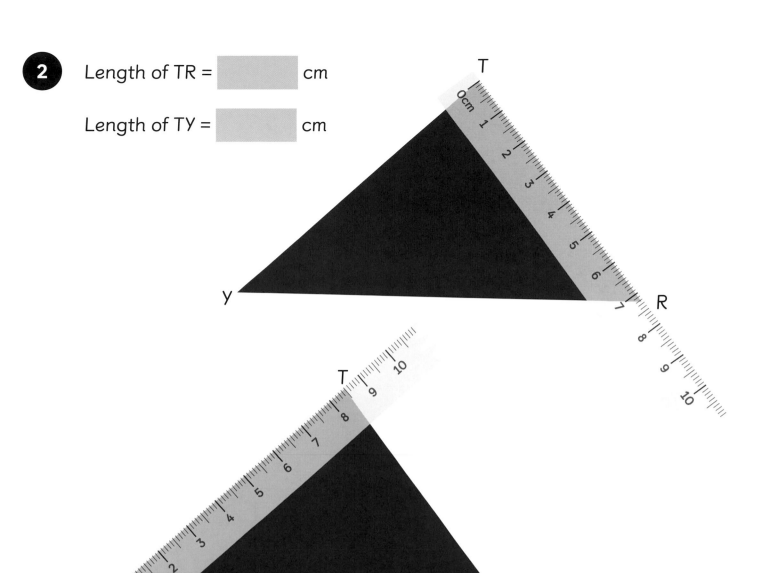

10 + 7 + 8 = 25

The perimeter is definitely longer than 20 cm.

You only need to know RY = 10.7 cm. With that, you can conclude that the perimeter is more than 20 cm.

Can you see why?

Guided Practice

1 Measure the length of each side.

(a)

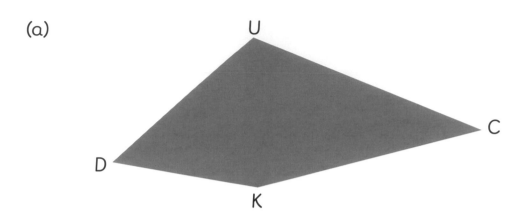

(b)

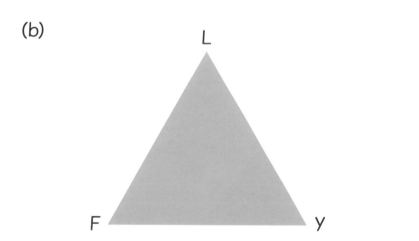

(c)

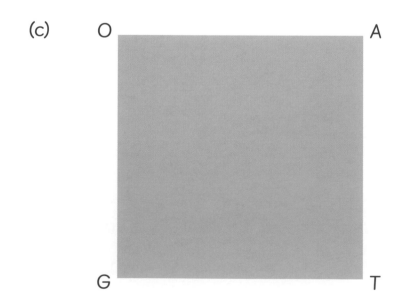

2 (a) Draw a square that has a perimeter of about 20 cm.

   (b) Draw a triangle that has a perimeter of about 20 cm.

3 Measure each side to the nearest cm.

Estimate the perimeter.

Is your estimate longer or shorter than the actual perimeter? Why?

Complete Worksheet **8** – Page **79 - 80**

Converting Units of Length

In Focus

This table shows how far six athletes jumped.

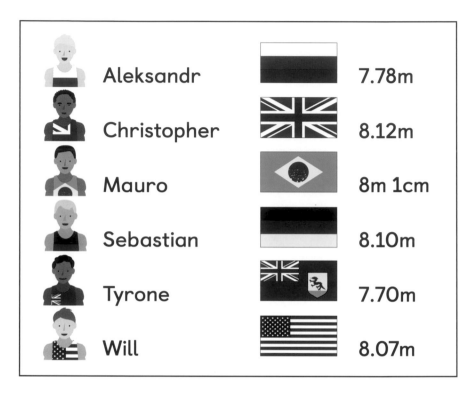

Aleksandr		7.78m
Christopher		8.12m
Mauro		8m 1cm
Sebastian		8.10m
Tyrone		7.70m
Will		8.07m

Who jumped further, or ?

Let's Learn

1 Which distance is longer, 8 m 1 cm or 8.10 m?

1 m = 100 cm

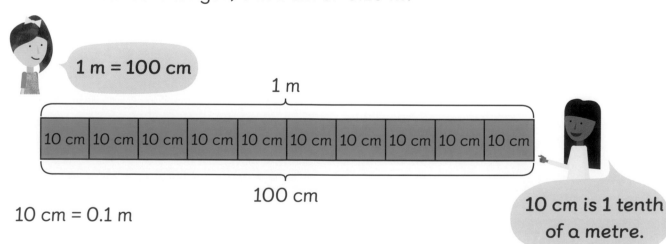

10 cm = 0.1 m

10 cm is 1 tenth of a metre.

So, 8.10 m is 8 m 10 cm.

That's longer than 8 m 1 cm.

8.10 m > 8 m 1 cm

2 8.10 m = [　　　] cm

$$1 \text{ m} = 100 \text{ cm}$$
$$8 \text{ m} = 800 \text{ cm}$$
$$\underline{0.10 \text{ m} = 10 \text{ cm}}$$
$$8.10 \text{ m} = 810 \text{ cm}$$

3 8.12 m = [　　　] m [　　　] cm

100 cm = 1 m

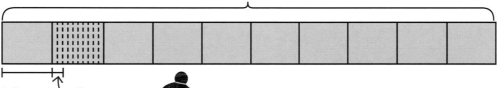

10 cm ⌐2 cm

2 cm = 2 hundredths of a metre

10 cm = 1 tenth of a metre

10 cm = 0.1 m

8.12 m = 8 m 12 cm

 4 8.12 m = [　　　] cm

$$1 \text{ m} = 100 \text{ cm}$$
$$8 \text{ m} = 800 \text{ cm}$$
$$0.1 \text{ m} = 10 \text{ cm}$$
$$\underline{0.02 \text{ m} = 2 \text{ cm}}$$
$$8.12 \text{ m} = 812 \text{ cm}$$

5

I jumped 8 m and 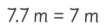 cm.

I jumped 7 m and cm.

7.7 m = 7 m [ ] cm

8.07 m = 8 m [ ] cm

0.1 m = 10 cm
0.7 cm = 70 cm

0.01 m = 1 cm
0.07 cm = 7 cm

1 m	= 100 cm
7 m	= 700 cm
0.7 m	= 70 cm
7.7 m	= 770 cm

1 m	= 100 cm
8 m	= 800 cm
0.7 m	= 7 cm
8.07 m	= 807 cm

Guided Practice

1 How far did each person jump?

	Distance
	4.10 m
	4.01 m
	3.90 m
	3.92 m
	3.02 m

Give your answers in centimetres.

I jumped [ ] cm.

2 This table shows the distance jumped by four athletes.

Position	Name		Distance
1st	Greg		8.31 m
2nd	Mitchell		8.16 m
3rd	Will		8.12 m
4th	Michel		8.11 m

(a) Greg beat Mitchell for the gold medal by [   ] cm.

8.31 = 8 m [   ] cm   8.16 m = 8 m [   ] cm

(b) Michel lost the bronze medal to Will by [   ] cm.

8.12 m = 8 m [   ] cm   8.11 m = 8 m [   ] cm

Complete Worksheet **9** – Page **81 - 82**

Converting Units of Length

In Focus

After 20 minutes of a 10-km race:

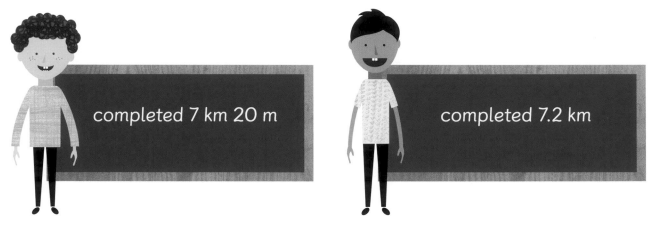

completed 7 km 20 m

completed 7.2 km

Who was ahead in the race after 20 minutes, or ?

Let's Learn

1   10 km = [   ] m

10 km = 10 000 m

1 km = 1000 m

10 km = 10 000 m

2 7.2 km = [ ] m

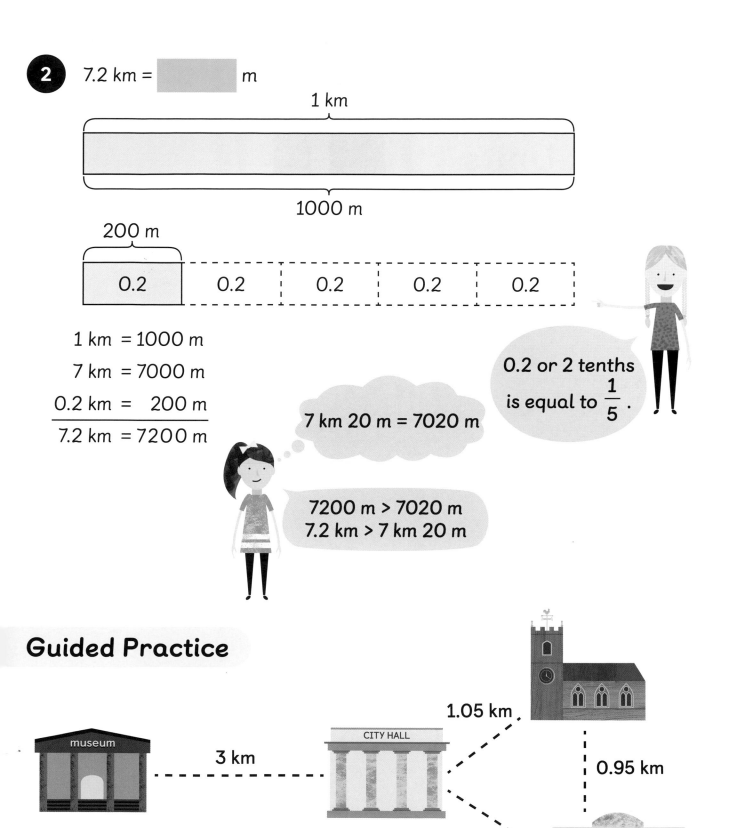

1 km

1000 m

200 m

| 0.2 | 0.2 | 0.2 | 0.2 | 0.2 |

1 km = 1000 m
7 km = 7000 m
0.2 km =   200 m
7.2 km = 7200 m

7 km 20 m = 7020 m

0.2 or 2 tenths is equal to $\frac{1}{5}$.

7200 m > 7020 m
7.2 km > 7 km 20 m

Guided Practice

museum

3 km

CITY HALL

1.05 km

0.95 km

1.3 km

Station

How far is each place to the others in metres?

Complete Worksheet **10** – Page **83 – 84**

Measuring Perimeter in Different Units

In Focus

I measured all four sides. The perimeter is 16.

I measured only two sides. The perimeter is 160.

Explain how they got their answers.

Let's Learn

1 measured all four sides in cm.

5 cm

3 cm

3 cm

5 cm

Perimeter = 3 cm + 5 cm + 3 cm + 5 cm

= 16 cm

2 × 3 cm = 6 cm
2 × 5 cm = 10 cm

2 measured two sides in mm.

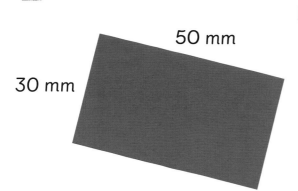

50 mm

30 mm

Perimeter = 2 × 30 mm + 2 × 50 mm

= 60 mm + 100 mm

= 160 mm

1 cm = 10 mm
16 cm = 160 mm

Guided Practice

1 Measure each perimeter.

(a)

(b)

(c)

Give your answers in mm and in cm.

2 The lengths of the sides of three rectangles are measured and recorded on the diagrams.

(a)

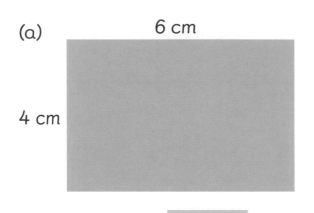

6 cm

4 cm

Perimeter = ___ mm

(b)

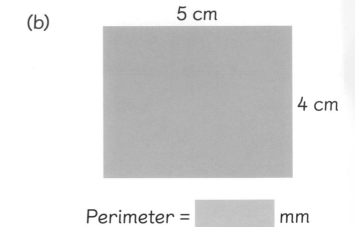

5 cm

4 cm

Perimeter = ___ mm

(c)

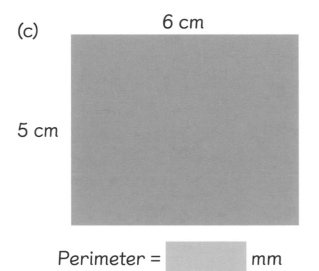

6 cm

5 cm

Perimeter = ___ mm

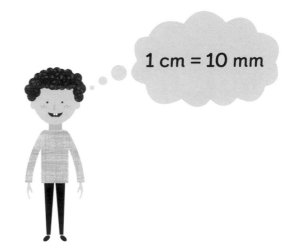

1 cm = 10 mm

Complete Worksheet **11** – Page **85 – 87**

Solving Problems Involving Scale Reading

In Focus

Pumpkin Bar Recipe

– 1 cup vegetable oil
– 2 cups flour
– 4 eggs
– 15 oz pumpkin puree

I am using 12 eggs to make some pumpkin bars.

How much flour and vegetable oil does need?

Let's Learn

1 How much flour is needed?

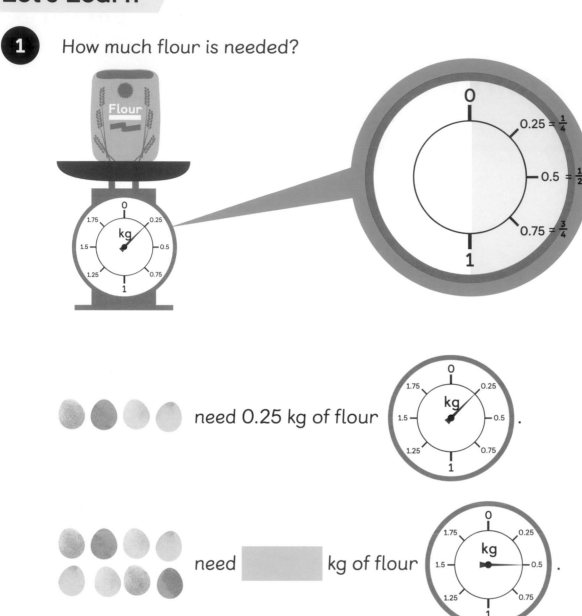

need 0.25 kg of flour .

need ____ kg of flour .

need ____ kg of flour .

2 How much oil is needed?

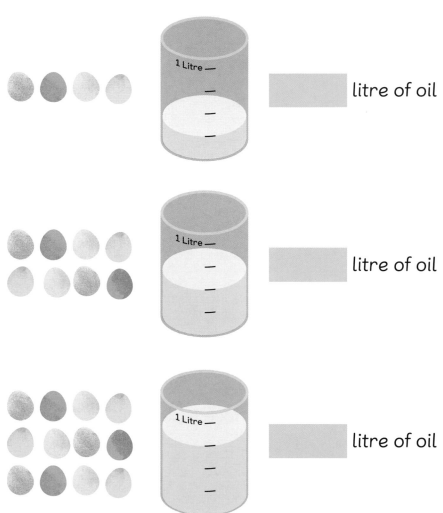

_____ litre of oil

_____ litre of oil

_____ litre of oil

Guided Practice

1 Read the scale.

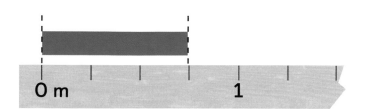

0 m ———————— 1

Name something that is that long.

2 This man is 0.85 m taller than his son. Find his son's height.

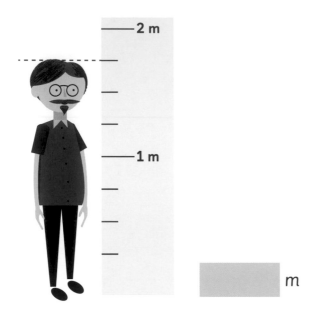

[   ] m

3 A second box is 0.25 kg lighter than this box. A third box is 0.5 kg heavier than this box. Find the total mass of the three boxes.

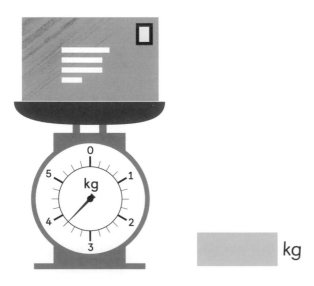

[   ] kg

Complete Worksheet **12** – Page **88 – 89**

You are provided a tap, an empty container and two measuring containers. One measuring container has a marking for 400 ml and the other 1.5 l. There are no other marking on the containers.

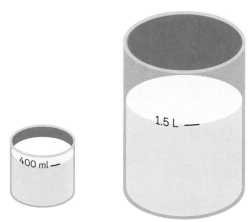

Explain how you can measure out these volume of water:

(a)   100 ml

(b)   300 ml

Maths Journal

Ten £1 coins are put on a weighing scale.

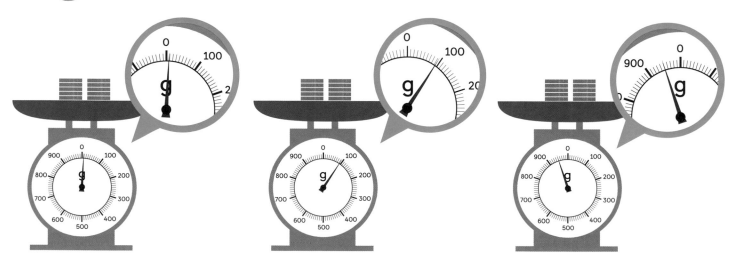

Which of these is most likely the reading on the scale?

Explain how you arrive at your conclusion.

I know how to...

☐ measure and estimate mass.

☐ measure and estimate volume.

☐ measure and estimate length.

☐ convert units of mass.

☐ convert units of volume.

☐ convert units of length.

☐ measure perimeter in different units.

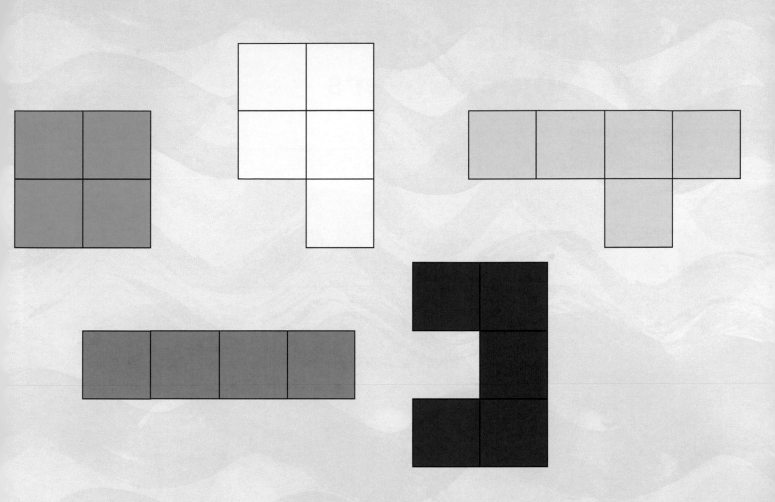

If you want to make these, which one uses the most paper?

Chapter 11
Area of Figures

Measuring the Surface that an Object Covers

In Focus

Compare how much surface the photograph covers with how much surface the square tile covers.

Let's Learn

1. The surface the photograph covers is 8 times the surface 1 of the square tiles covers.

2 Which figure covers more surface?

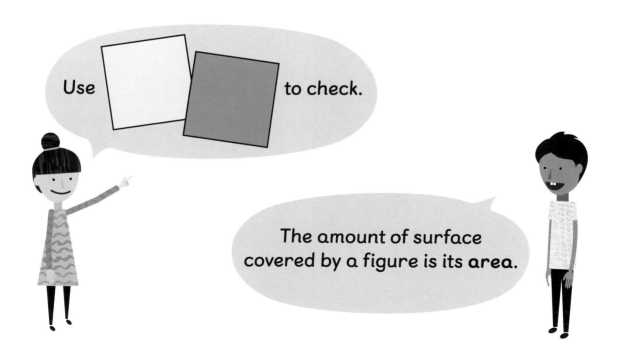

1 Estimate how much surface is covered by each figure.

Measure it using .

The surface covered by this figure is ☐ times the surface covered by 1 square tile.

Complete Worksheet **1** – Page **103 - 104**

Measuring Area

In Focus

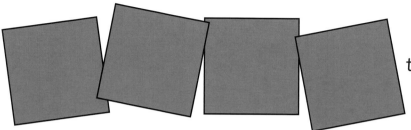

Use to make as many different figures as you can.

You do not need to use all four tiles.

Let's Learn

 1 uses .

 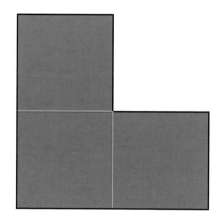

Each figure covers the same amount of surface as 3 square tiles.

Each figure has the same area as 3 square tiles.

2  uses .

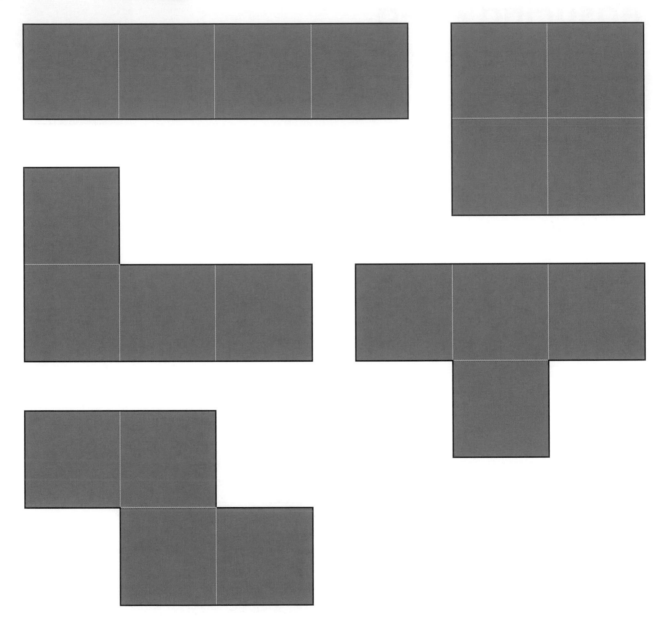

Each figure covers the same amount of surface as 4 square tiles.

The area of each figure is equal to the area of the 4 square tiles.

Work in groups of 3 or 4.

What you need:

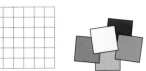

① Make a figure using
5 square tiles.

② Make as many figures as
you can. All the figures must have the same area.

③ Draw the figures on [grid] .

Guided Practice

Use square tiles to form these figures.

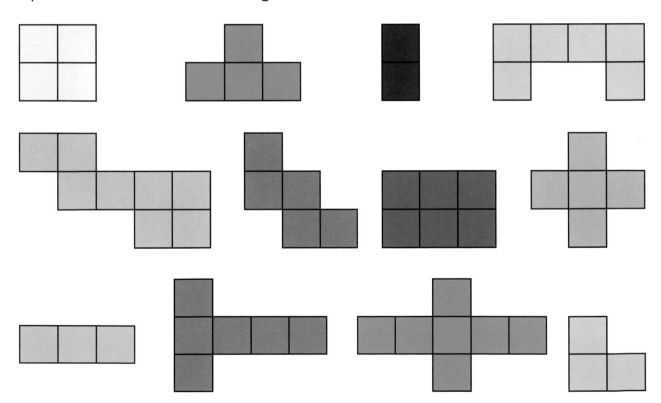

Sort the figures according to area.

Complete Worksheet 2 – Page 105 - 106

Measuring Area

In Focus

Figures with the same area can have different perimeters.

Figures with the same perimeter can have different areas.

Who is correct?

Let's Learn

1 Make different figures with the same area and the same perimeter.

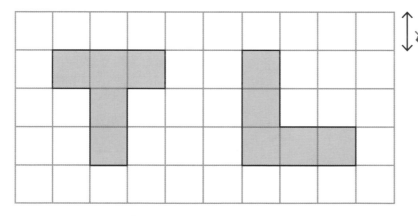

Let this be 1 unit.

perimeter = 12 units
    area = 5 square units

perimeter = 12 units
    area = 5 square units

We say the area of is 1 square unit.

2 Make figures with the same area but different perimeters.

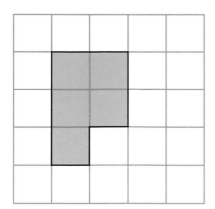

perimeter = 10 units
    area = 5 square units

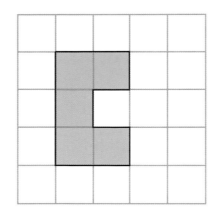

perimeter = 12 units
    area = 5 square units

3 Make figures with different areas but the same perimeter.

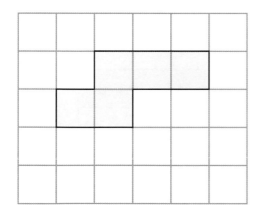

perimeter = 12 units
    area = 5 square units

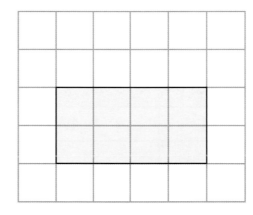

perimeter = 12 units
    area = 8 square units

Area measures the amount of surface inside a shape.

Perimeter measures the length around a figure.

These are different measures of size.

Work in groups of 3 or 4.

What you need:

① Use  to make some figures.

Use 6 for each figure.

② Label each figure.

③ Record the area and the perimeter of the figures.

Example:

Make sure the sides
of the touch
one another.

Figure	Area (square units)	Perimeter (units)
1	10	22

What do you notice about the area and the perimeter
of each figure?

1. Given that 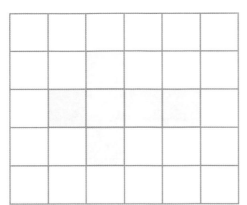 is 1 unit, find the area and the perimeter of this figure.

2. Draw two figures on the grid paper so that they have the same perimeter but different areas.

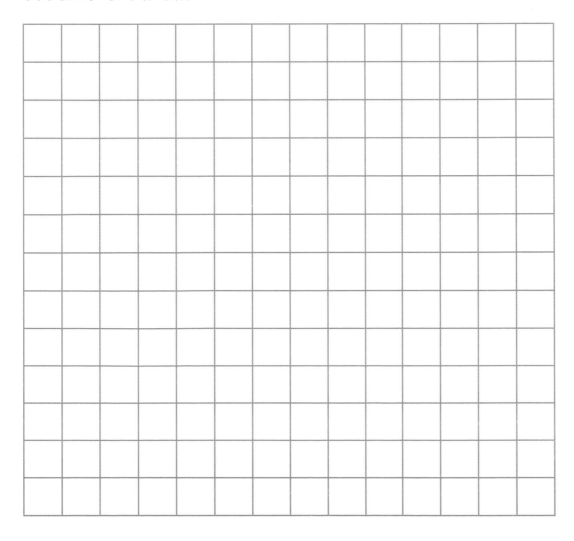

3 Find the area of each figure.

(a) Area of A = 2 square units

(b) Area of B = ☐ square units

(c) Area of C = ☐ square units

(d) Area of D = ☐ square units

(e) Area of E = ☐ square units

(f) Area of F = ☐ square units

Complete Worksheet 3 – Page 107 - 108

Measuring Area

In Focus

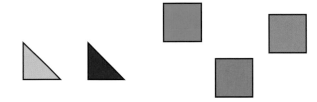

Make different figures using all 5 pieces.

Let's Learn

 1 makes this.

Its area is 4 square units.

has an area of 1 square unit.

 2 makes this.

Its area is 4 square units.

It can also be written as 4 units^2.

3 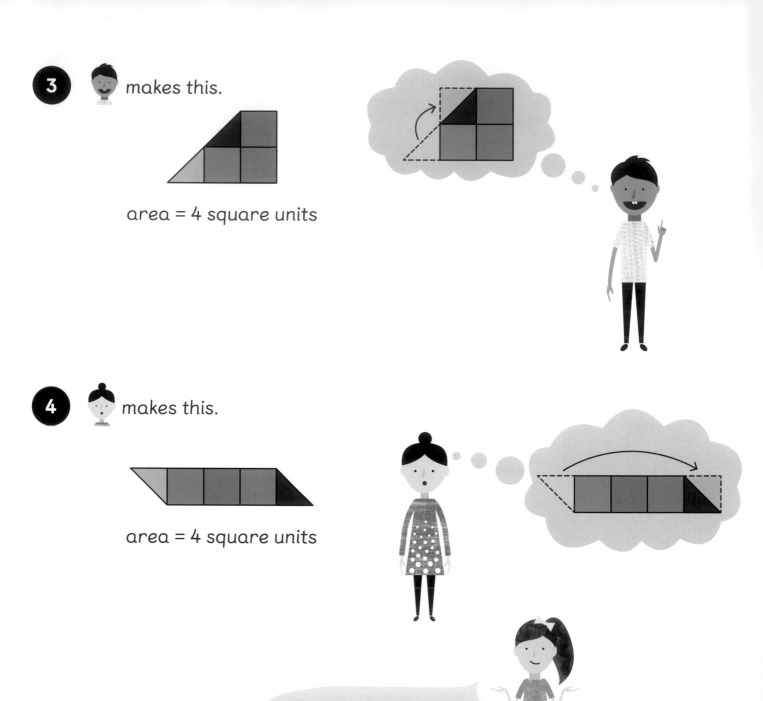 makes this.

area = 4 square units

4 makes this.

area = 4 square units

Can you tell who made
the figure with the
longest perimeter?

Find the area of each figure. ☐ has an area of 1 square unit.

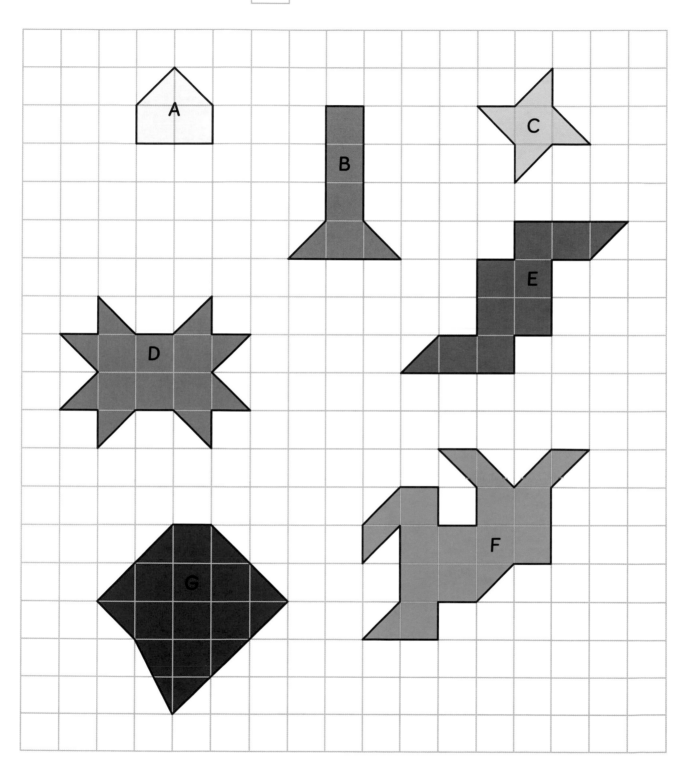

Complete Worksheet 4 – Page **109 - 110**

Measuring Area

In Focus

 drew some rectangles.

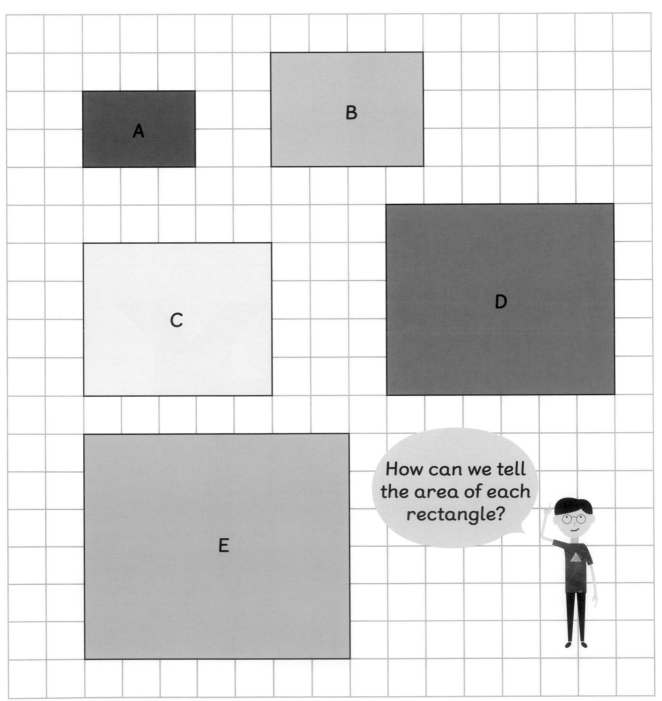

How can we tell the area of each rectangle?

1

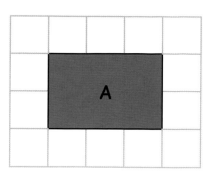

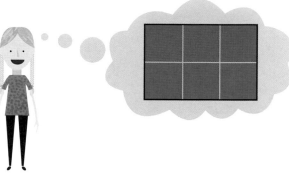

3 square units in 1 row

There are 2 rows.

$2 \times 3 = $

The area of Rectangle A is 6 square units.

2

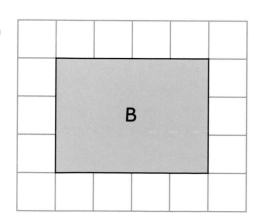

4 square units in 1 row

There are 3 rows.

$3 \times 4 = $

The area of Rectangle B is 12 square units.

3

5 square units in 1 row

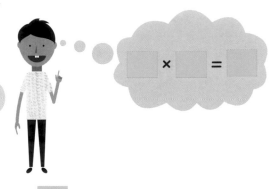

There are 4 rows.

The area of Rectangle C = ⬜ square units

4 Complete the table.

Rectangle	Area
A	6 square units
B	⬜ square units
C	⬜ square units
D	⬜ square units
E	⬜ square units

What do you think the area of Rectangle H would be?

 thinks that all these rectangles form part of a sequence / pattern.

Can you explain the pattern?

Find the area of each square and each rectangle.

I count squares.

I use multiplication.

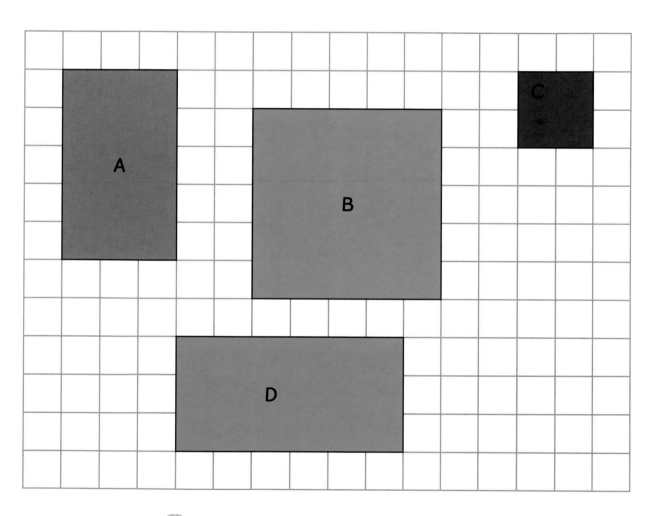

(a) Use 's method.

(b) Use 's method.

Complete Worksheet 5 – Page 111 – 112

Measuring Area

In Focus

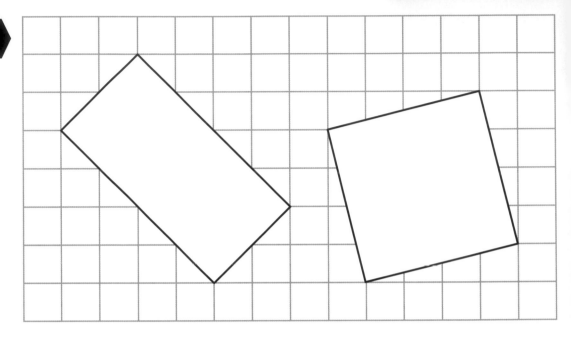

Which has the larger area?

Let's Learn

1   Find the area of the first figure.

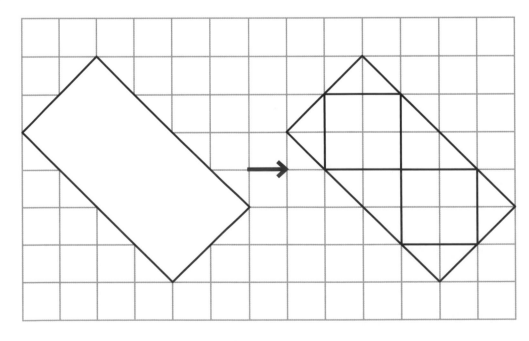

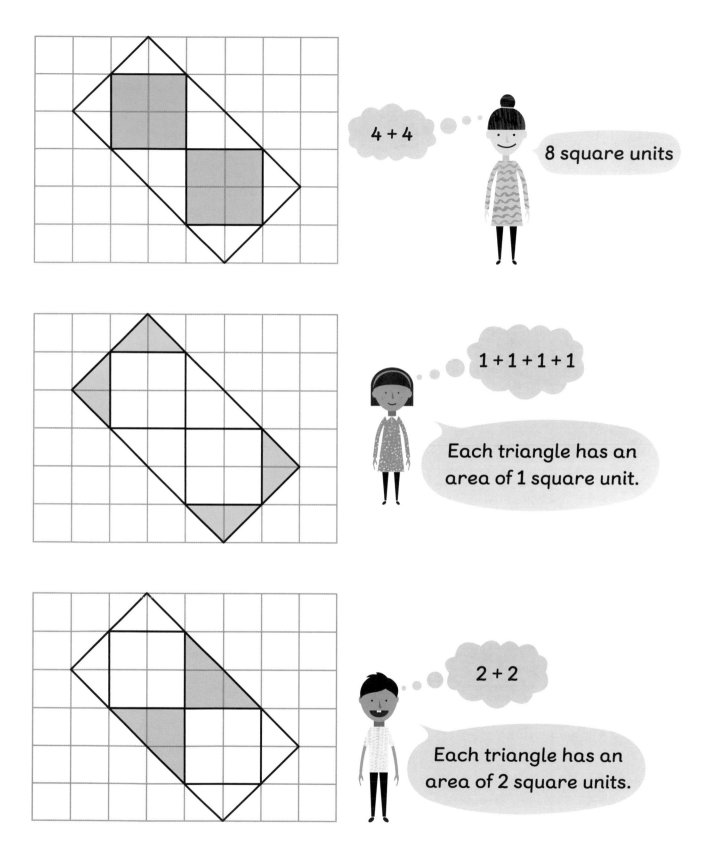

4 + 4

8 square units

1 + 1 + 1 + 1

Each triangle has an area of 1 square unit.

2 + 2

Each triangle has an area of 2 square units.

The first figure has an area of 16 square units.

2 Find the area of the second figure.

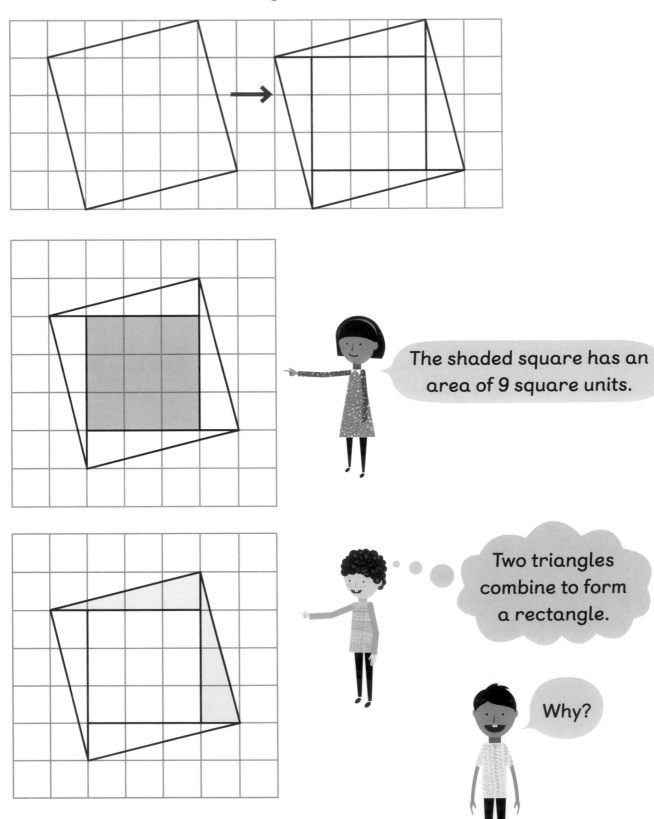

The shaded square has an area of 9 square units.

Two triangles combine to form a rectangle.

Why?

The second figure has an area of 17 square units.

The area of square A is 1 square unit.

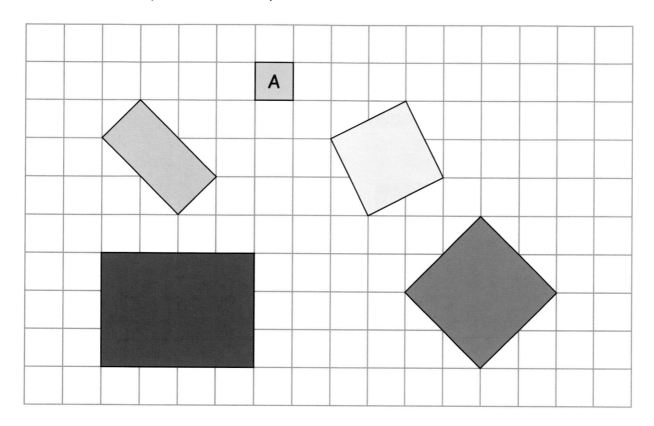

Find the area of the other figures.

Complete Worksheet **6** – Page **113 – 114**

This square has an area of 4 square units.

 thinks it is possible to find the area of these squares.

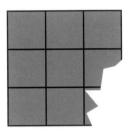 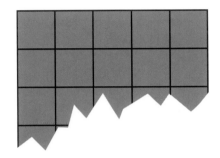 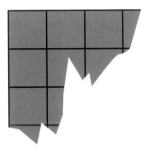

Is correct?

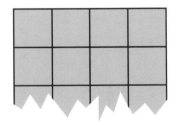 thinks it is possible to find the area of these rectangles.

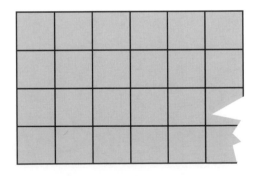 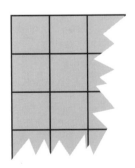

Is correct?

Maths Journal

 cuts a rectangular piece of paper into two identical pieces.

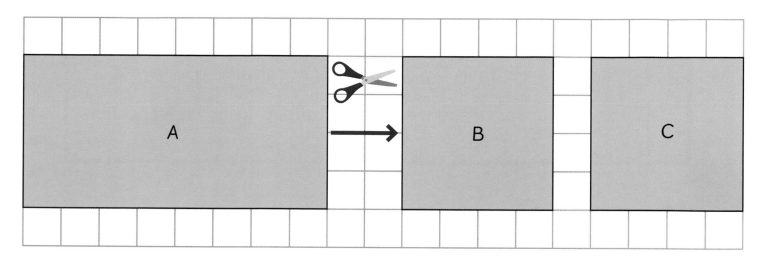

The total area of B and C is twice the area of A.

The total perimeter of B and C is twice the perimeter of A.

Explain why and are wrong.

I know how to...

☐ find the area of figures using square tiles.

☐ find the area and the perimeter of figures in a square grid.

☐ find the areas of squares and rectangles using multiplication.

Can you find these shapes in this book?

Chapter 12
Geometry

Knowing Types of Angles

In Focus

Look for acute angles, right angles and obtuse angles in the triangles.

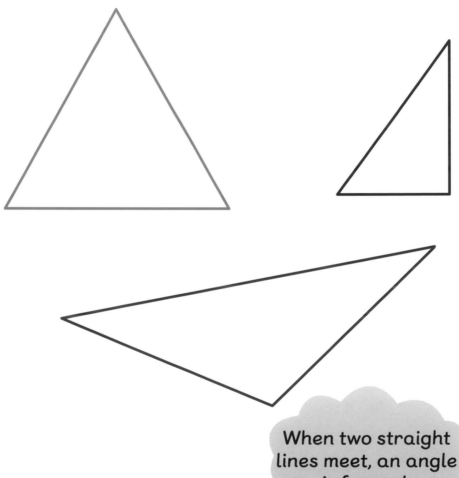

When two straight lines meet, an angle is formed.

Draw a quadrilateral that has all three types of angles.

Let's Learn

1 Show acute angles.

Acute angles are less than a right angle.

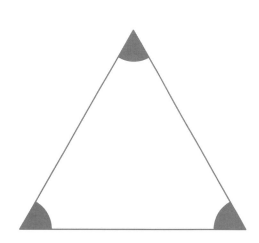

right angle

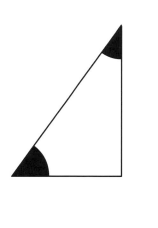

2 Show the right angle.

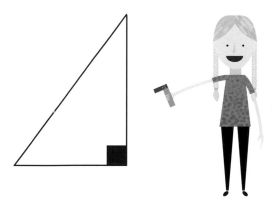

You can use a right-angle checker.

3 Show the obtuse angle.

Obtuse angles are more than a right angle but less than two right angles.

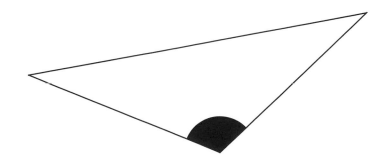

4 Show acute angles, obtuse angles and right angles in each quadrilateral.

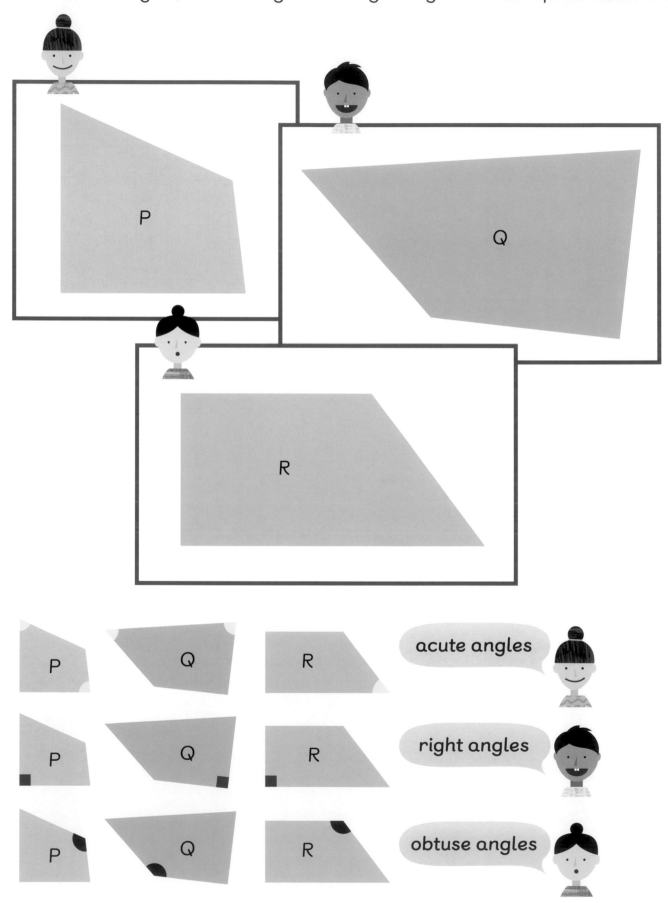

acute angles

right angles

obtuse angles

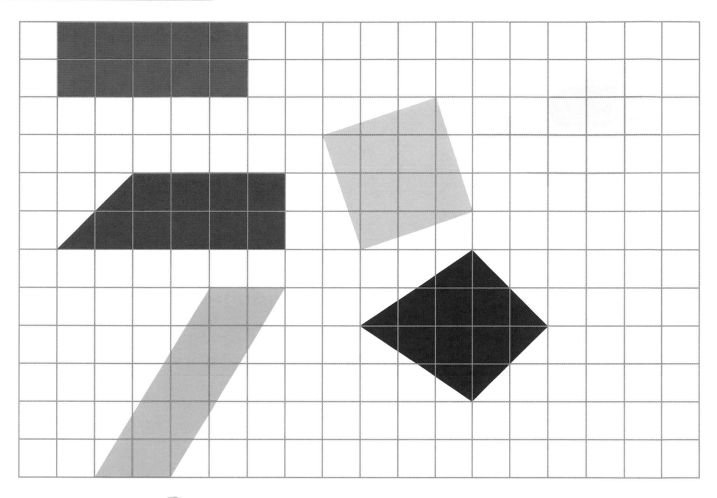

Which angles
are acute?

Which angles
are obtuse?

Use a right-angle
checker to help you.

Which angles are
right angles?

Complete Worksheet **1** – Page **121 - 122**

Comparing Angles

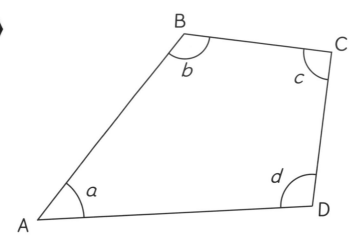

Compare the sizes of the four angles in Figure ABCD.

Let's Learn

1 Which angle is the smallest?

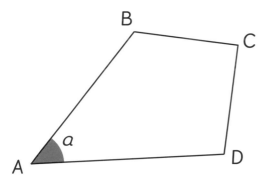

Angle *a* is less than a right angle.

2 Which angle is the largest?

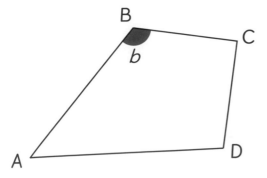

Angle *b* is more than a right angle.

3 Which angle is smaller, angle *c* or angle *d*?

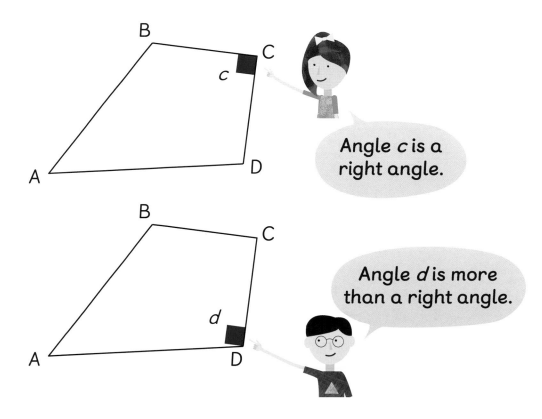

Angle *c* is a right angle.

Angle *d* is more than a right angle.

angle *a* < angle *c* < angle *d* < angle *b*

Can you explain why?

1 Which angle is larger?

(a)

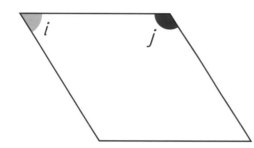

(b)

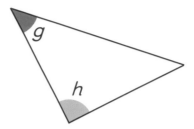

(c)

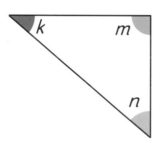

2 Arrange the angles from the smallest to the largest.

(a)

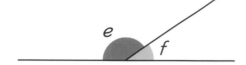

(b)

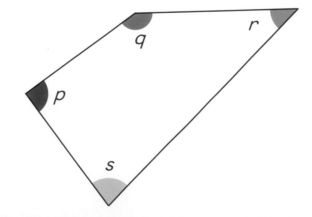

Complete Worksheet **2** – Page **123 – 125**

Classifying Triangles

In Focus

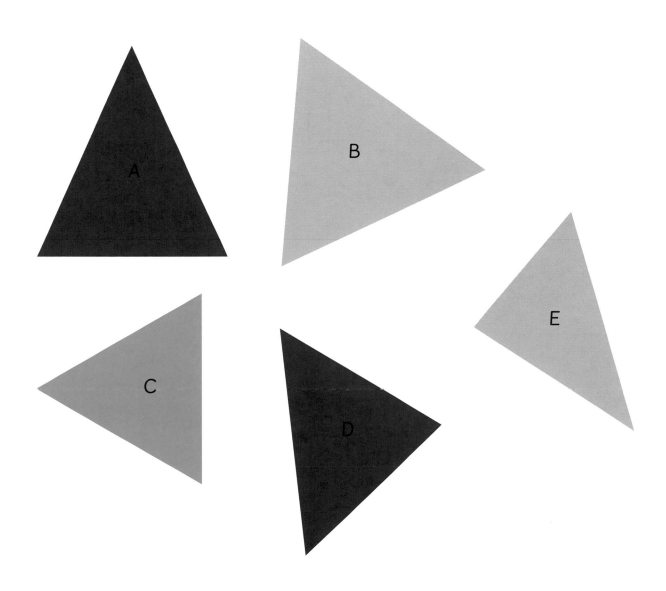

How are they alike?

How are they different?

1 looks at the lengths of the sides.

all three sides are of equal lengths	only two sides are of equal lengths	all three sides are of different lengths
B C	A D	E

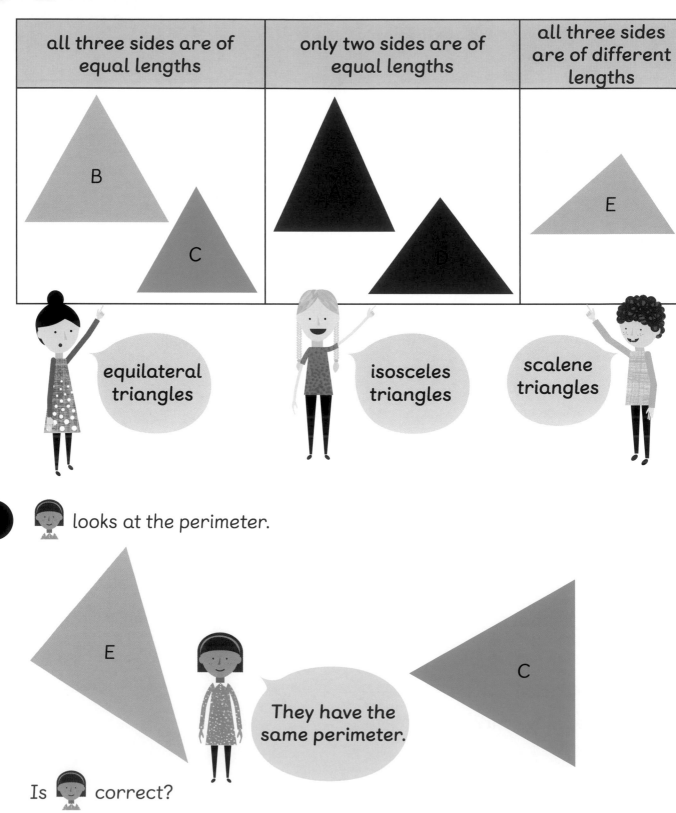

equilateral triangles

isosceles triangles

scalene triangles

2 looks at the perimeter.

E   C

They have the same perimeter.

Is correct?

1 In a scalene triangle, all three sides have different lengths.
Which of these are scalene triangles?

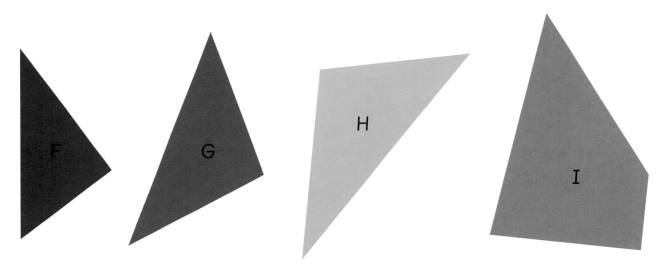

2 In an equilateral triangle, all three sides have the same length.
Which of these are equilateral triangles?

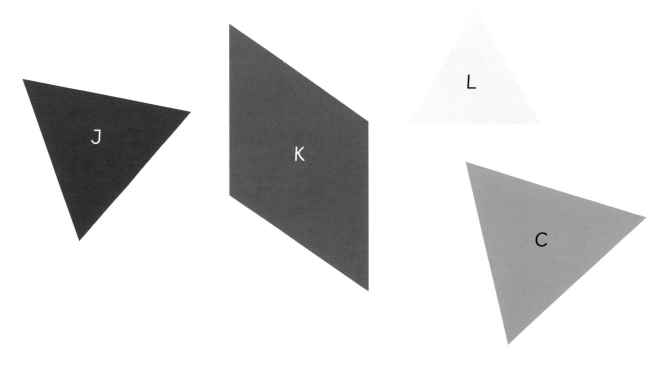

3 In an isosceles triangle, two sides are of equal lengths.

Which of these are isosceles triangles?

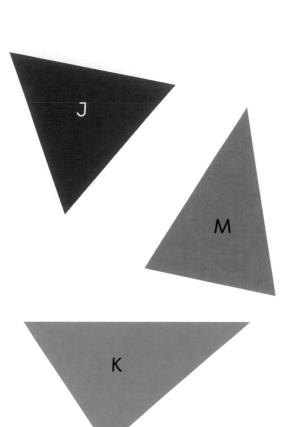

Draw another isosceles triangle.

Complete Worksheet **3** – Page **126 – 128**

Classifying Quadrilaterals

In Focus

Quadrilaterals are polygons with four sides.

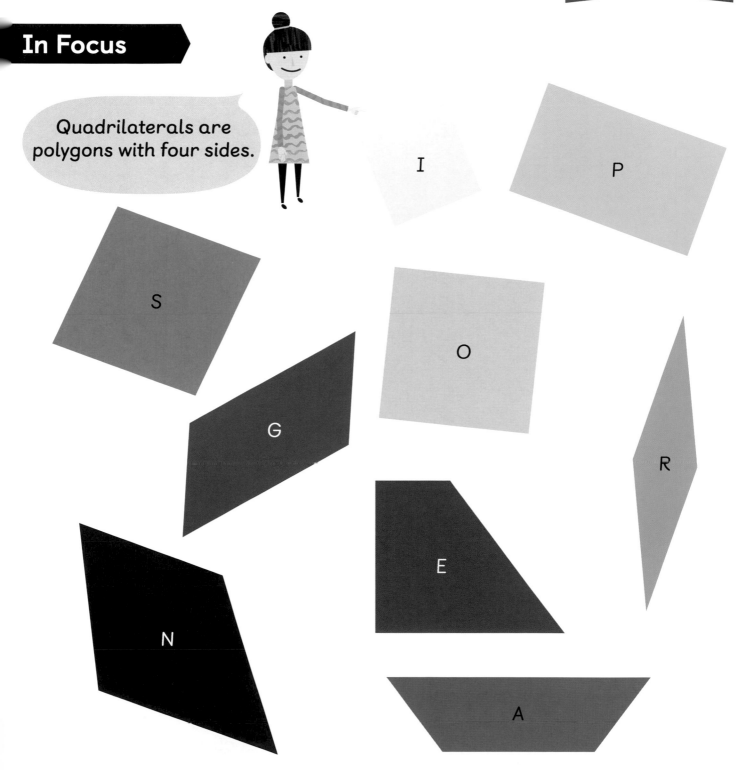

Look for similarities between quadrilaterals that allow you to put them into groups.

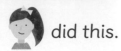

1 did this.

I put these four quadrilaterals into the same group because...

each has four equal sides.

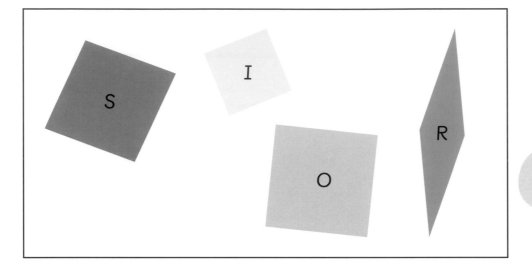

2 did this.

I put these three quadrilaterals into the same group because each has 4 right angles.

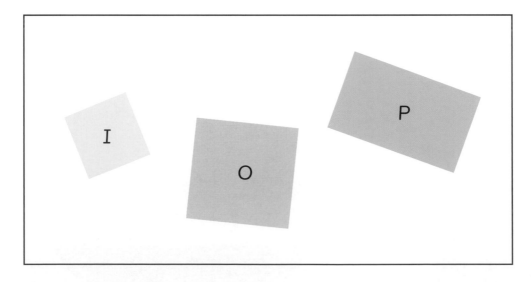

Look for similarities between quadrilaterals that allow you to put them into groups.

3 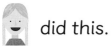 did this.

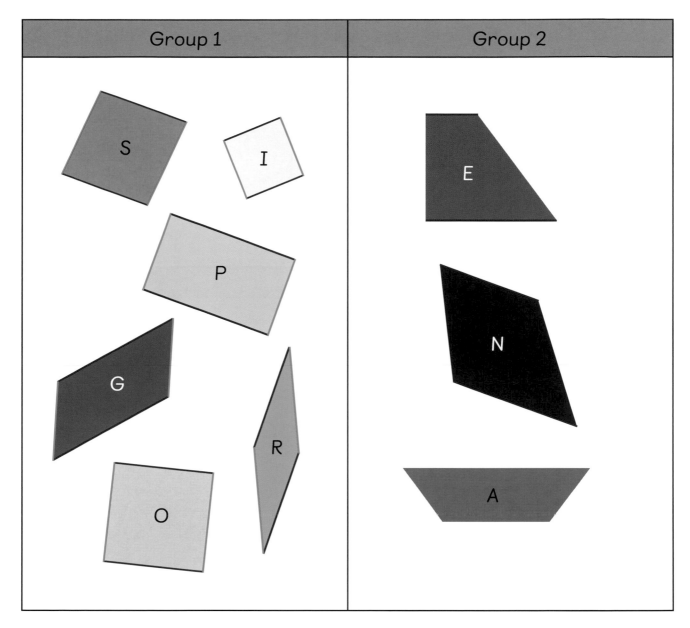

Group 1	Group 2

What is 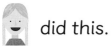's rule?

A quadrilateral with a pair of parallel sides is a **trapezium**.

4  did this.

rhombus	parallelogram
S R	G

square	rectangle
I	P

What makes a
quadrilateral a rhombus?

Guided Practice

1 Which of the following are squares?

Why?

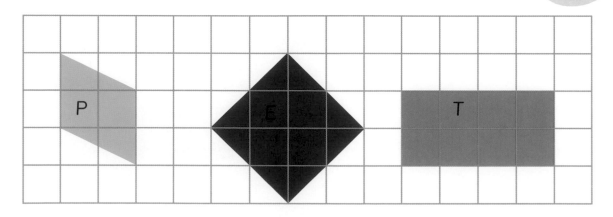

2 Which of the following are rectangles?

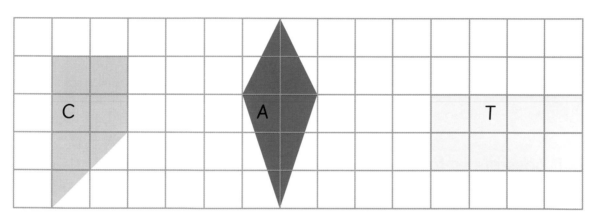

3 Which of the following are trapeziums?

4 Which of the following are parallelograms?

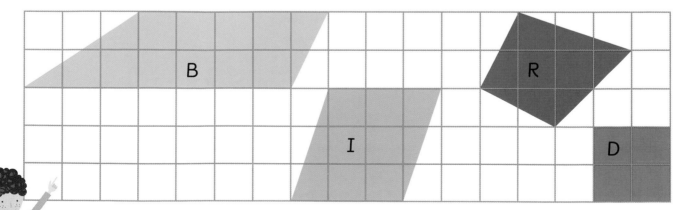

Are any of the quadrilaterals
on this page rhombuses?

Complete Worksheet **4** – Page **129 – 132**

Identifying Symmetrical Figures

In Focus

Is it possible to fold a square or a rectangle in half...

so that one half falls exactly on the other half?

Let's Learn

1  did this.

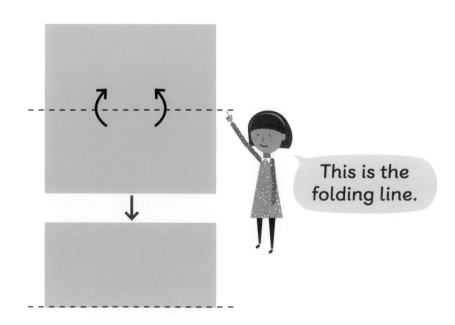

This is the folding line.

2 did this.

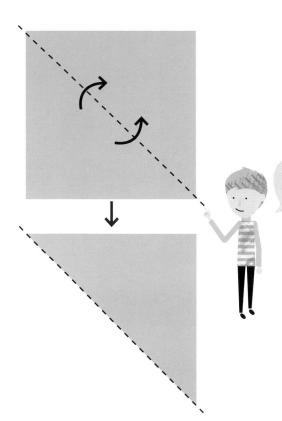

This is the folding line.

The two halves are identical.

A square is symmetrical.

Are there more folding lines for the square?

3 did this.

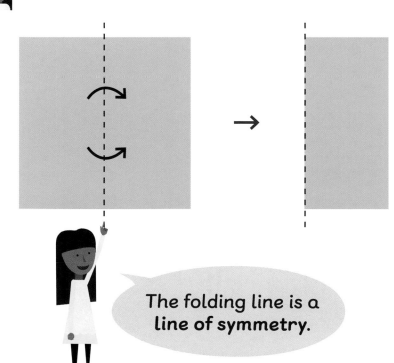

The folding line is a **line of symmetry.**

4  did this.

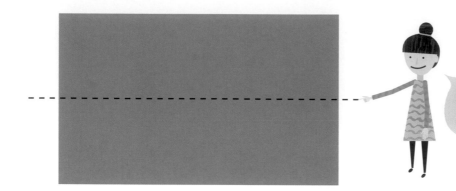

Is this a line of symmetry?

5  did this.

This is not a line of symmetry. Why not?

6  did this.

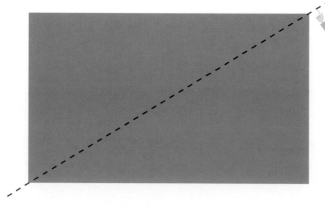 

Is this a line of symmetry?

Work in groups of 3 or 4.

① Cut out different shapes from  .

What you need:

② Try to fold each shape into two halves so that one half fits exactly on top of the other.

③ Draw the line of symmetry if the shape is symmetrical.

④ Put the shapes into two groups.

symmetrical figures	non-symmetrical figures

Guided Practice

1 Which of the following are symmetrical?

2 Show a line of symmetry in each figure.

Complete Worksheet **5** – Page **133**

Drawing Lines of Symmetry

In Focus

Does this figure have lines of symmetry?

How many?

Let's Learn

1 drew this line.

 The two halves match up exactly.

2 drew this line.

The top half is a reflection of the bottom half. The two halves are reflections of each other along the line of symmetry.

3 drew this line.

 How many lines of symmetry does have?

Why is this not a line of symmetry?

1 Find a line of symmetry in each figure.

(a)

(b)

(c)

(d)

Can you find how many lines of symmetry each figure has?

2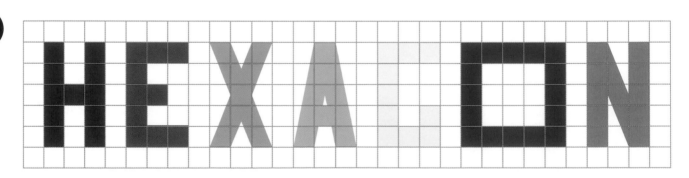

(a) Which letters have 1 line of symmetry?

(b) Which letters have 2 lines of symmetry?

(c) Which letters have more than 2 lines of symmetry?

(d) Which letters have no lines of symmetry?

Complete Worksheet 6 – Page 134 – 137

Completing Symmetrical Figures

In Focus

This is one half of a symmetric figure. What does the complete figure look like?

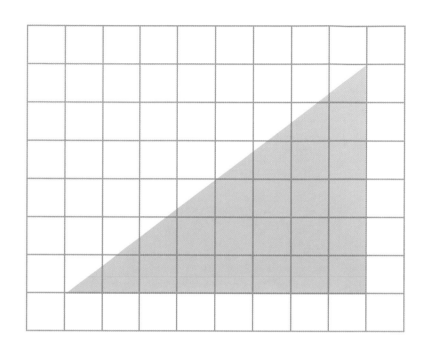

Let's Learn

1 thinks that this is the line of symmetry.

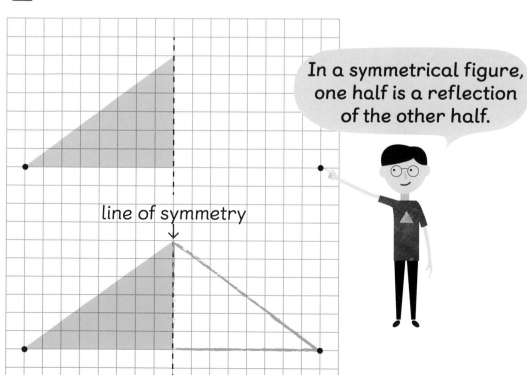

line of symmetry

In a symmetrical figure, one half is a reflection of the other half.

thinks that this is the line of symmetry.

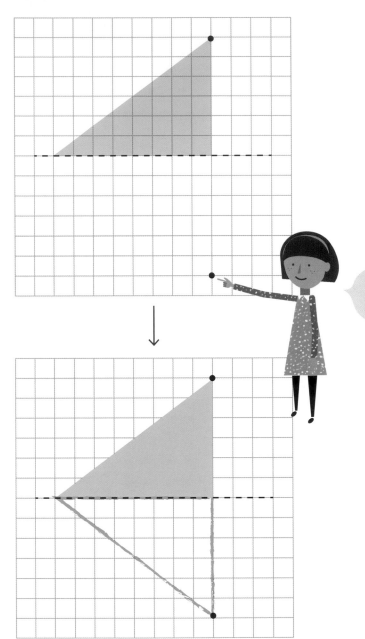

Mark a point here.

Complete each symmetrical figure.

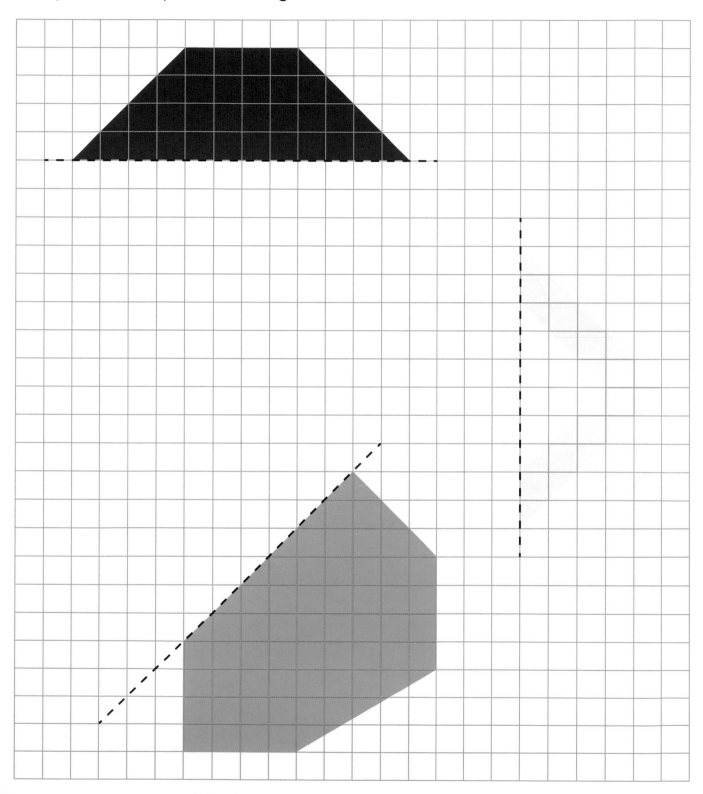

Complete Worksheet **7** – Page **138 – 140**

Making Symmetrical Figures

In Focus

 puts some paint on a square piece of paper.

He folds the paper along one of the lines of symmetry.

What does the paper look like afterwards?

① Put on some paint.

↓

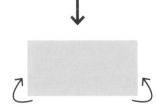

② Fold along a line of symmetry.

↓

③ Open it up.

Let's Learn

1 What if folds it this way?

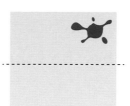

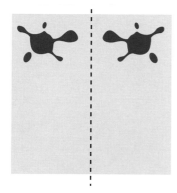

2 What if folds it this way?

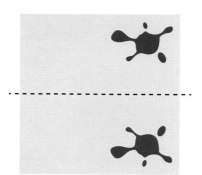

3 What if folds it this way?

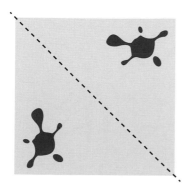

Guided Practice

Draw the line of symmetry to show how the sheet on the left can be folded to make the one on the right.

is wet paint.

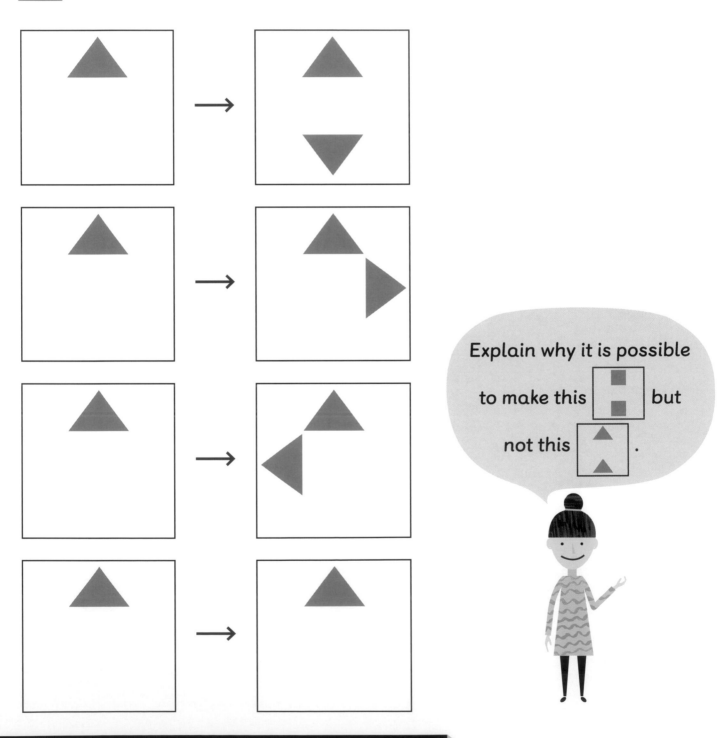

Explain why it is possible to make this [▪ / ▪] but not this [▲ / ▲].

Complete Worksheet 8 – Page **141 - 142**

Completing Symmetrical Figures

In Focus

Make the figure symmetrical by adding more and .

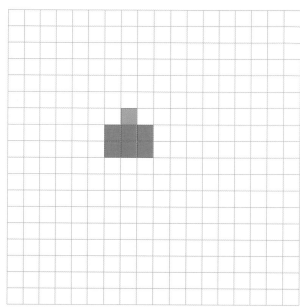

Let's Learn

1 did this.

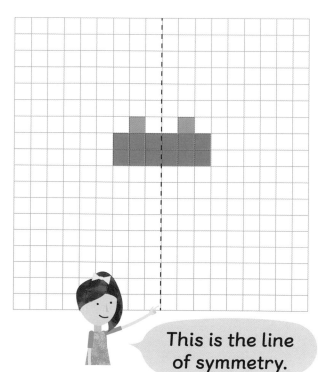

This is the line of symmetry.

2 did this.

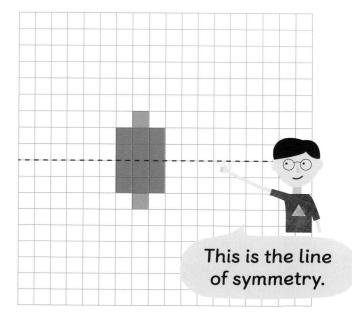

This is the line of symmetry.

3   did this.

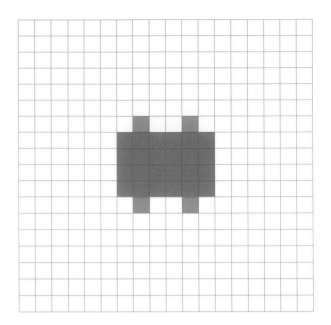

Is this figure symmetrical?

Where is the line of symmetry?

Is there more than
one line of symmetry?

4   did this.

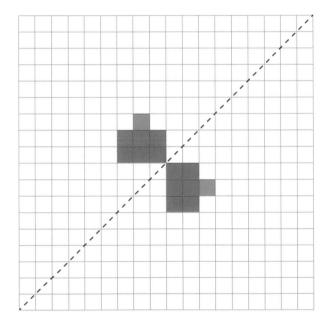

Is this figure symmetrical?

Where is the line of symmetry?

1 Make each pattern symmetrical about the dotted line.

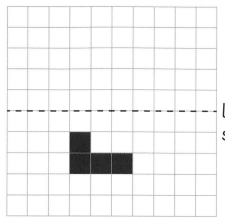 line of symmetry

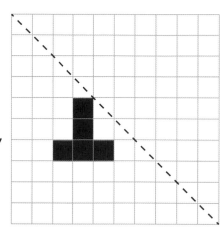 line of symmetry

2 Complete the figure so that it is symmetrical about the line – – – – – – .

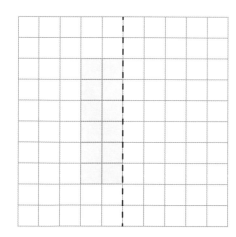

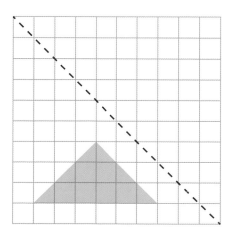

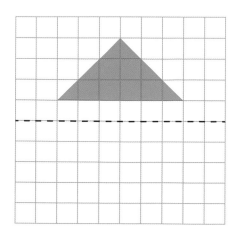

Complete Worksheet 9 – Page 143 – 144

Sorting Shapes

In Focus

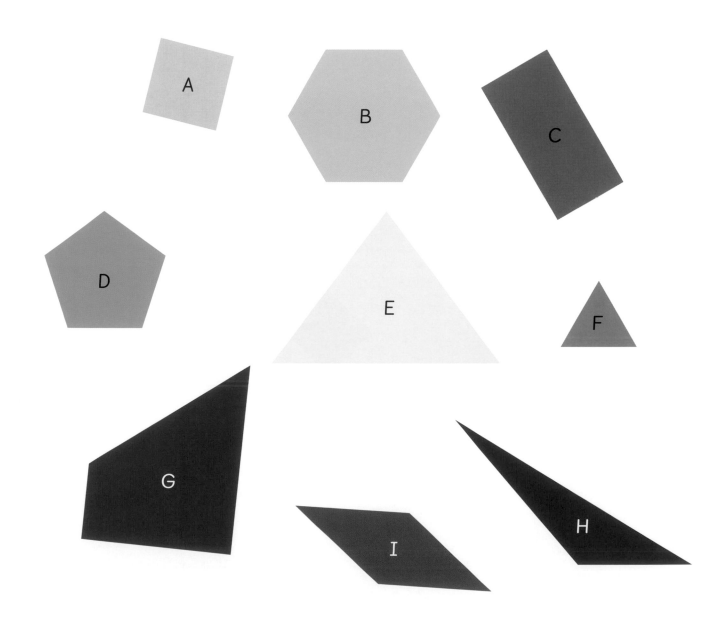

Classify the shapes into groups.

Explain how you do it.

1 classifies the shapes according to the number of sides.

triangles	quadrilaterals
F E H	A C G I

2 groups the shapes in terms of equal sides.

all sides are equal	not all sides are equal
A B D F I	C E G H

 A polygon with all sides equal and all angles equal is called **regular polygon**.

3   groups the polygons with at least one line of symmetry.

symmetrical figures	non-symmetrical figures
A B C F D E I	G H

 Can you show a line of symmetry for the symmetrical figures?

4 groups the polygons with an obtuse angle.

has at least one obtuse angle	no obtuse angle
B D G H I	A C E F

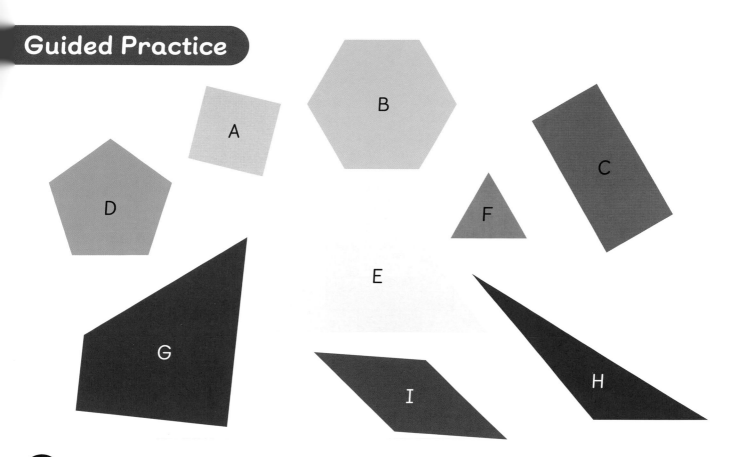

1. (a) Name a quadrilateral that has only 2 lines of symmetry.

   (b) Name a quadrilateral that has 4 lines of symmetry.

   (c) Name a quadrilateral that has no line of symmetry.

2. Measure the polygons with a ruler. Group those that have the same perimeter.

3. Classify some of the polygons according to their angles.

has at least one right angle	no right angle

Can you draw a triangle that belongs to this group?

Complete Worksheet 10 – Page 145 – 146

Half of each figure is shown.

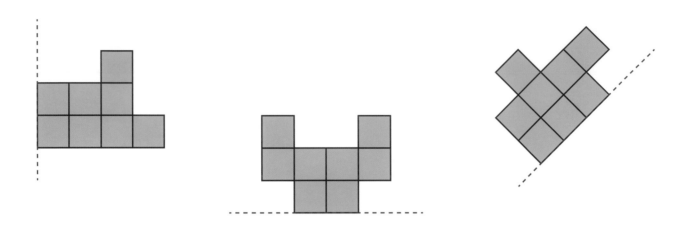

Use any two of these pieces to complete each symmetrical figure.

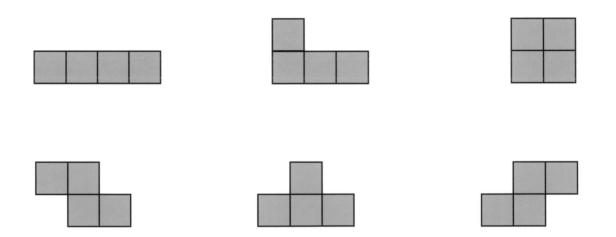

Each piece may be used for more than one figure.

Measure all the sides of each polygon.

A regular polygon has more than one line of symmetry.

A regular polygon is one with all its sides equal and all its angles equal.

Is it true?

Explain in your journal. Give examples.

I know how to...

☐ identify acute and obtuse angles.

☐ compare and order angles.

☐ compare and classify triangles and quadrilaterals.

☐ identify lines of symmetry in 2-D shapes.

☐ complete a simple symmetrical figure with respect to a specific line of symmetry.

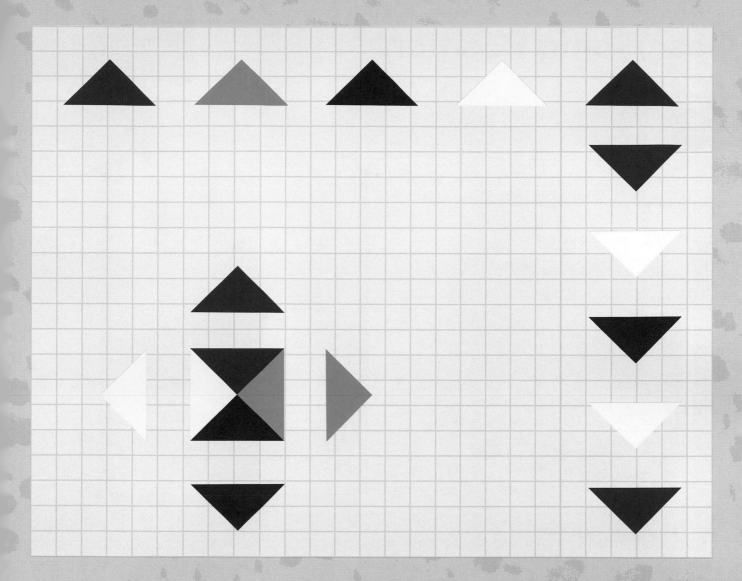

Can you describe how the triangles move to make this pattern?

Chapter 13
Position and Movement

Describing Position

In Focus

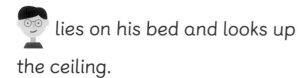 lies on his bed and looks up the ceiling.

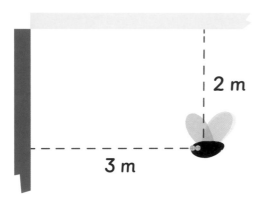

2 m

3 m

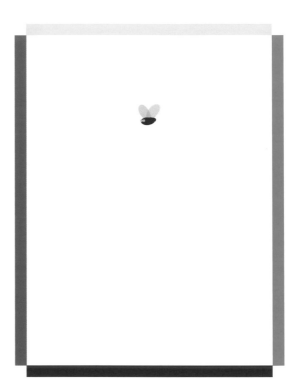

This is what I see lying on the bed.

How can Charles tell the exact position of the fly?

1 How far is the fly from the walls?

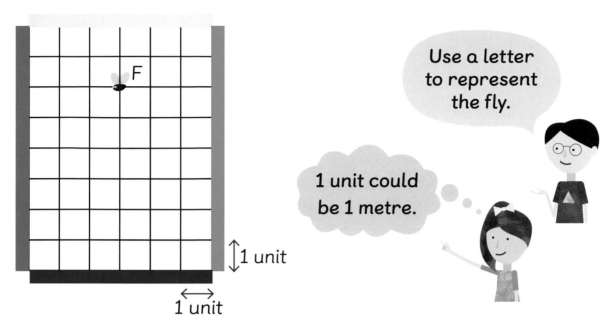

Use a letter to represent the fly.

1 unit could be 1 metre.

1 unit

1 unit

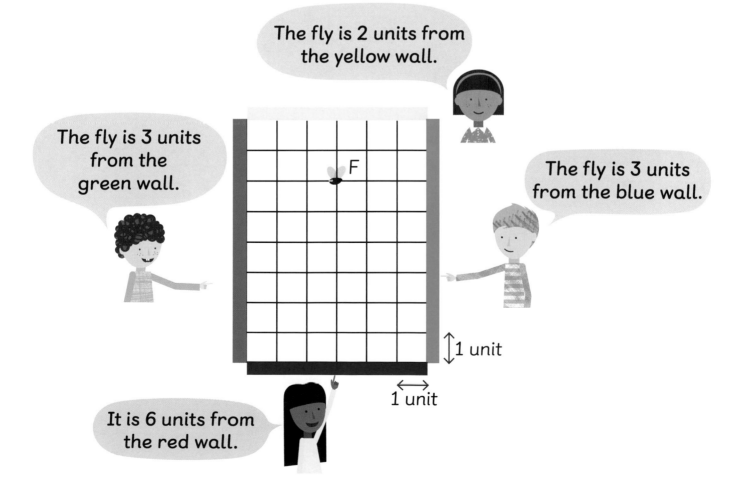

The fly is 2 units from the yellow wall.

The fly is 3 units from the green wall.

The fly is 3 units from the blue wall.

It is 6 units from the red wall.

1 unit

1 unit

2 What do you think of their suggestions?

How far is the fly from the red wall?

The fly is 6 units from the red wall and 2 units from the yellow wall.

 The fly is 3 units from the green wall and 3 units from the blue wall.

I think Charles must say how far the fly is from all four walls.

I don't think it is necessary to say how far the fly is from all four walls.

F

1 unit

1 unit

Guided Practice

1 Several tourist attractions are surrounded by four major roads.

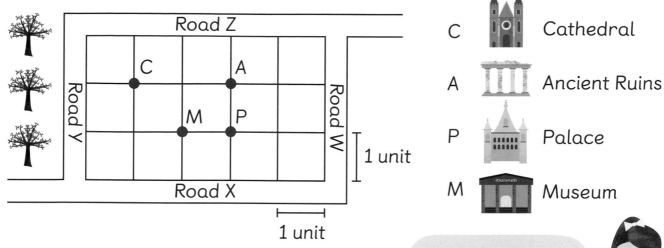

C Cathedral

A Ancient Ruins

P Palace

M Museum

In this case, 1 unit could be 1 km.

Describe the location of each tourist attraction by describing its distance from the roads.

2 Describe the position of the vertices of the triangle.

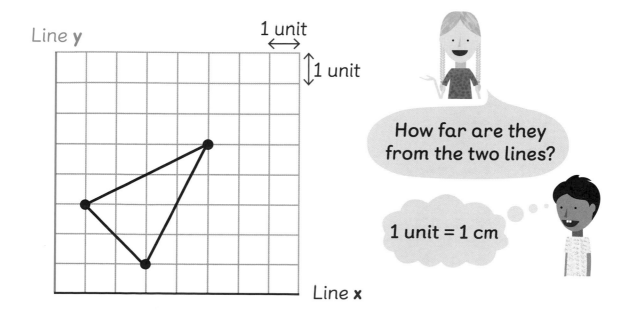

How far are they from the two lines?

1 unit = 1 cm

Complete Worksheet **1** – Page **151 – 154**

Describing Position

In Focus

Charles invents a way to describe the position of the fly.

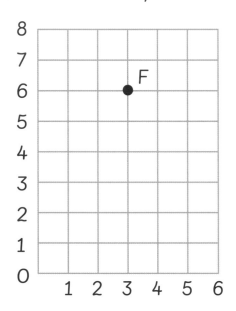

F =

F is at (3,6).

What does the 3 refer to?

What does the 6 refer to?

Explain Charles' method. What does (3,6) mean?

Let's Learn

These numbers show the distance from the x-axis.

We call this line the x-axis.

F is 6 units from the x-axis.

We write F = (, 6)

2

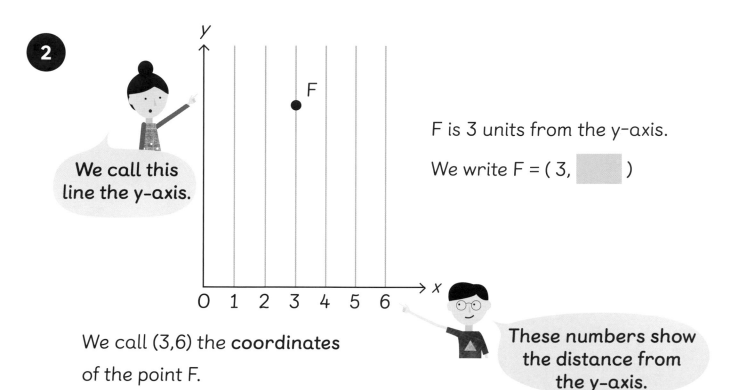

We call this line the y-axis.

F is 3 units from the y-axis.

We write F = (3, [ ])

These numbers show the distance from the y-axis.

We call (3,6) the **coordinates** of the point F.

Guided Practice

1 Using coordinates, describe the positions of a bee, B; a spider, S; and a fly; F.

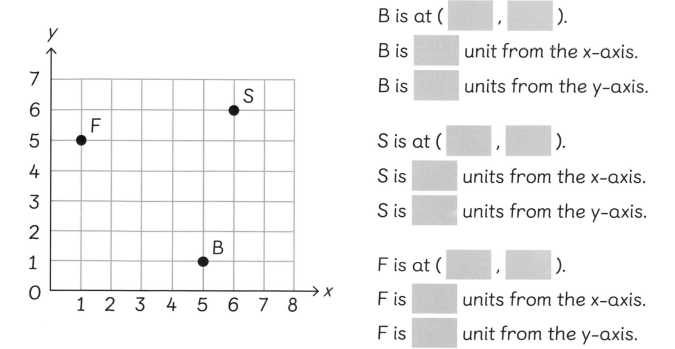

B is at ([ ] , [ ]).

B is [ ] unit from the x-axis.

B is [ ] units from the y-axis.

S is at ([ ] , [ ]).

S is [ ] units from the x-axis.

S is [ ] units from the y-axis.

F is at ([ ] , [ ]).

F is [ ] units from the x-axis.

F is [ ] unit from the y-axis.

A moth, M, is at (3,4). Is it closest to B, to S or to F?

2 A quadrilateral has vertices P, Q, R and S.

P is at (1,5)

Q is at (5,5)

R is at (5,1)

S is at (3,1)

What type of quadrilateral is PQRS?

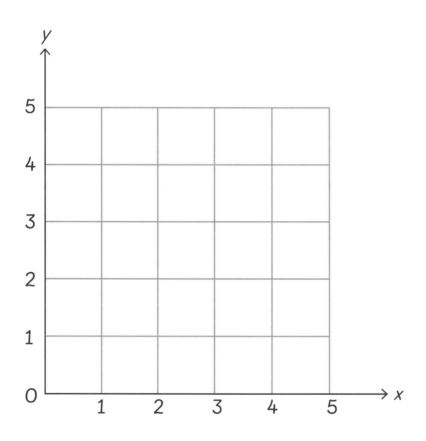

Draw PQRS on the grid.

Complete Worksheet **2** – Page **155 – 158**

Plotting Points

In Focus

Elliott has plotted three points.

Where should D be in order for ABCD to be a square?

Could ABCD be a quadrilateral with one line of symmetry?

Could ABCD be a rectangle?

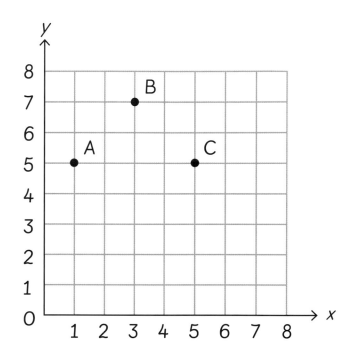

What if ABCD is a trapezium?

Let's Learn

1 ABCD is a square.

D is at (3,3).

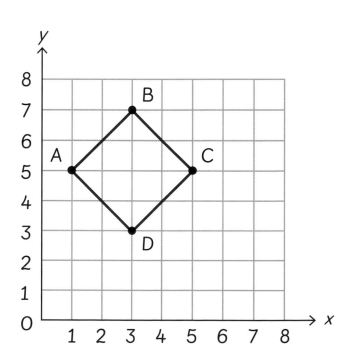

2 ABCD is a trapezium.

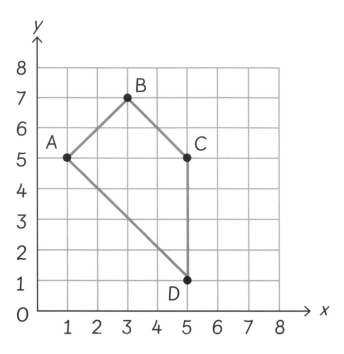

D is at (5 ,   ).

D is at (0,0).

Are there other ways to make ABCD a trapezium?

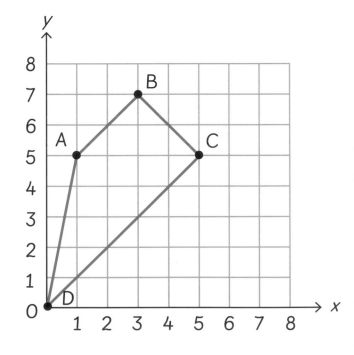

3 ABCD has one line of symmetry.

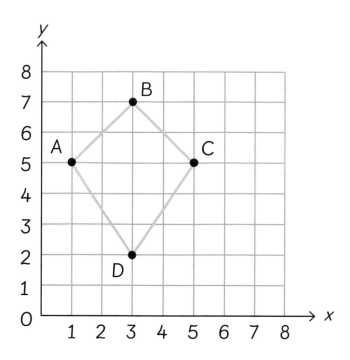

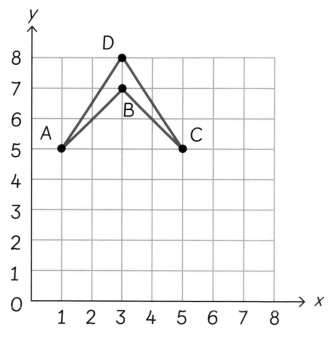

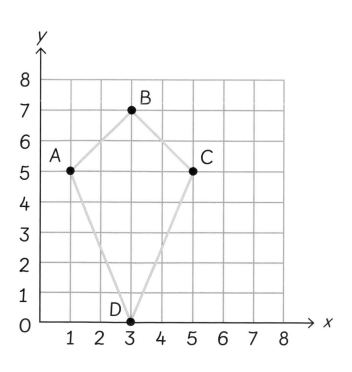

D is at (___ , ___).

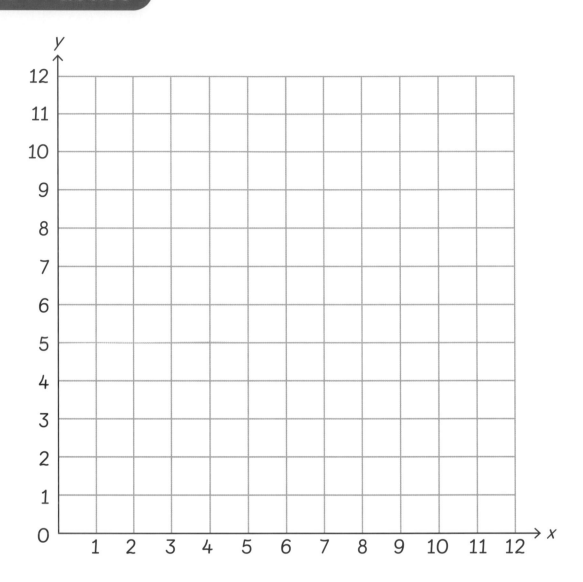

Draw each quadrilateral.

(a)   ABCD   A (1,2), B (2,3), C (3,2), D (2,1)

(b)   EFGH   E (1,5), F (3,5), G (4,6), H (2,6)

(c)   JKLM   J (4,10), K (6,9), L (4,8), M (2,9)

(d)   PQRS   P (5,3), Q (9,3), R (7,5), S (7,1)

(e)   TUVW   T (8,6), U (9,7), V (11,5), W (10,4)

What kind of quadrilateral is each of these?

Complete Worksheet 3 – Page **159 – 160**

Describing Movements

In Focus

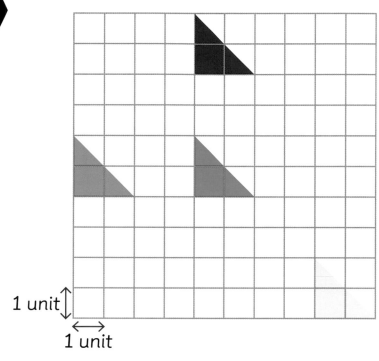

1 unit ↕

1 unit ↔

Describe how can move into each of the three positions.

Let's Learn

1 Describe 's movement into the position shown by .

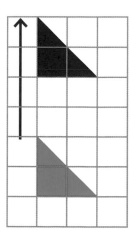

It moves up by 4 units.

2   Describe this movement.

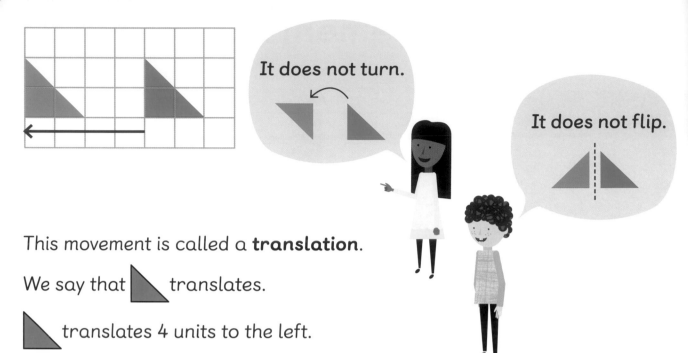

This movement is called a **translation**.

We say that 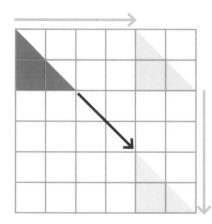 translates.

 translates 4 units to the left.

3   Describe this movement.

First translates 4 units to the right.

Then it translates 4 units downwards.

1

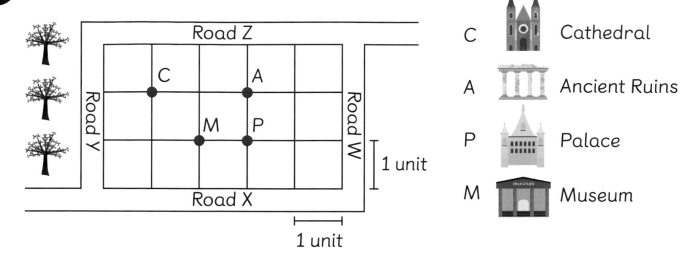

Describe the translation that can get a person from one place to another.

From	To
Cathedral	Ancient Ruins
Palace	Ancient Ruins
Palace	Museum
Cathedral	Palace
Museum	Ancient Ruins

2 The diagram shows the original position of .

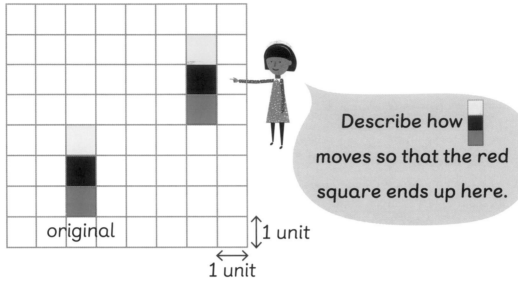

Describe how moves so that the red square ends up here.

1 unit

1 unit

Show where ends up after each translation is finished.

(a) moves up by 3 units.

(b) moves to the right by 4 units.

(c) moves to the left by 2 units.

Complete Worksheet 4 – Page **161 – 163**

Describing Movements

In Focus

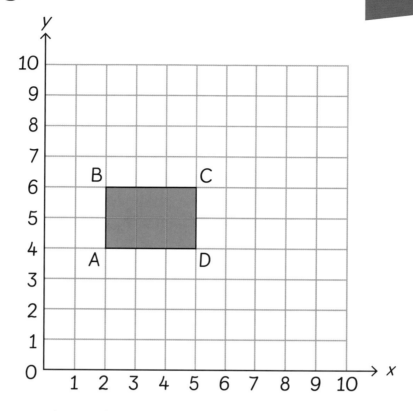

How can we move rectangle ABCD so that one of its vertices ends up at (7,8)?

Let's Learn

1

> Move it up 2 units and then 5 units to the right.

> Translate it 5 units to the right and then 2 units upwards.

Who is correct?

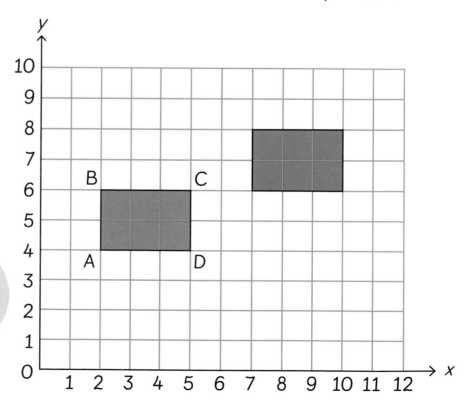

2

Translate it 4 units upwards and then 5 units to the right.

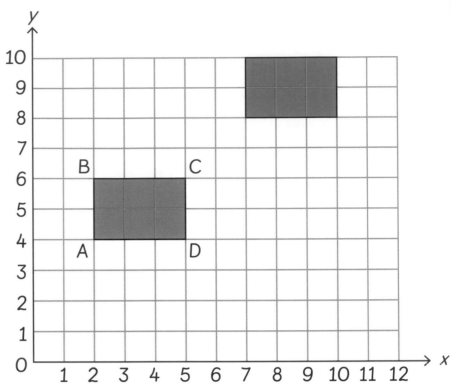

3

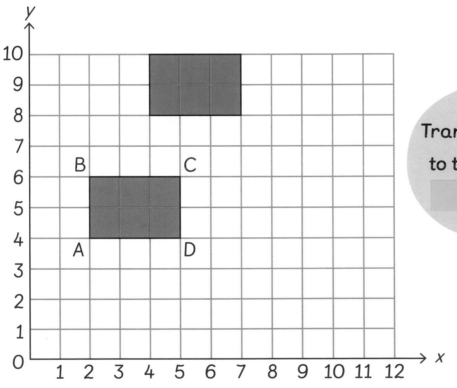

Translate it ___ units to the right and then ___ units upwards.

4

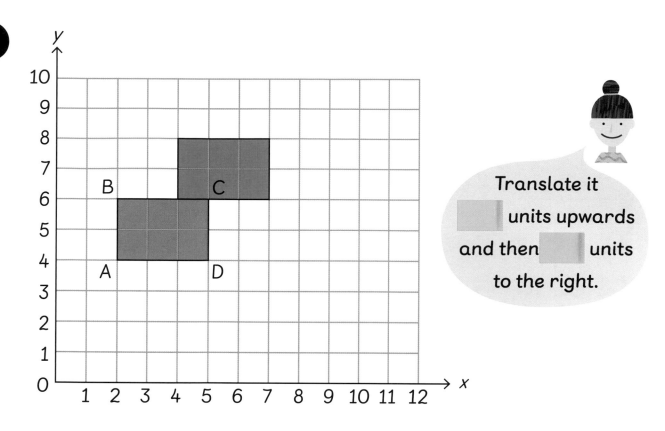

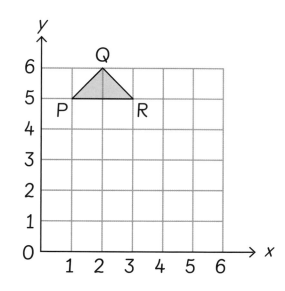

Translate it [ ] units upwards and then [ ] units to the right.

Guided Practice

Describe the translation that results in:

(a)   P being at (3,2).

(b)   Q being at (3,2).

(c)   R being at (3,2).

What are the coordinates of the other vertices?

Complete Worksheet **5** – Page **164 – 165**

How can we move rectangle ABCD so that one of its vertices ends up at (4,3)?

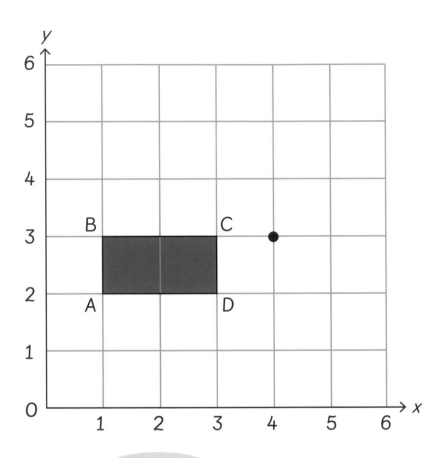

I translate the rectangle.

I turn the rectangle by one right angle.

I reflect the rectangle in a line of symmetry.

Show where the rectangle ends up in each case.

State the coordinates of A after the move.

Maths Journal

Sam draws a house by joining points with the coordinates shown on the right.
Create your own drawing using coordinates. Write a story to go with it.

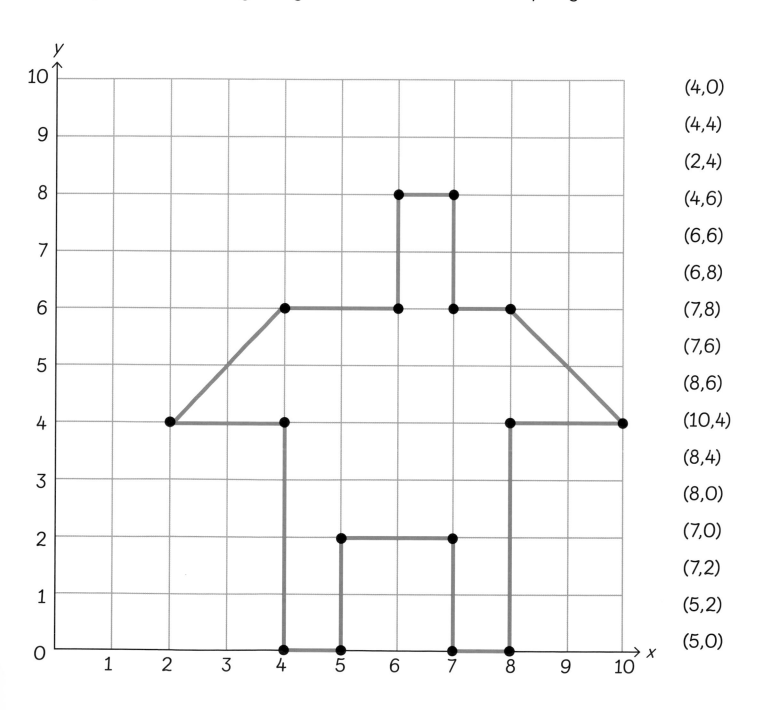

(4,0)

(4,4)

(2,4)

(4,6)

(6,6)

(6,8)

(7,8)

(7,6)

(8,6)

(10,4)

(8,4)

(8,0)

(7,0)

(7,2)

(5,2)

(5,0)

I know how to...

☐ describe positions using coordinates.

☐ plot points and form figures on the grid.

☐ describe movement including translation of figures.

Do we still use Roman numerals today?

Chapter 14
Roman Numerals

Writing Roman Numerals for 1 to 20

In Focus

The Romans used letters to write numbers. They used I for 1, V for 5 and X for 10.

Find out how the Romans wrote the numbers 1 to 20.

Let's Learn

1 Write the Roman numerals for 2, 3 and 20.

| I = 1 |
| II = 2 |
| III = 3 |

| X = 10 |
| XX = 20 |
| ? = 30 |

2 Write the Roman numerals for 6, 7 and 8.

| V = 5 |
| VI = 6 |
| VII = 7 |
| VIII = 8 |

V and I is 6.
five   one

V and II is 7.
five   two

V and III is 8.
five   three

3 Write the Roman numerals for 4 and 9.

V = 5
IV = 4

X = 10
IX = 9

I is before V.
IV is 1 less than 5.

I is before X.
IX is 1 less than 10.

4 Write the Roman numerals for the numbers 11 to 19.

10 = X	1 = I	11 = XI
10 = X	2 = II	12 = XII
10 = X	3 = III	13 = XIII
10 = X	4 = IV	14 = XIV
10 = X	5 = V	15 = XV
10 = X	6 = VI	16 = XVI
10 = X	7 = VII	17 = XVII
10 = X	8 = VIII	18 = XVIII
10 = X	9 = IX	19 = XIX

Guided Practice

1 Some watch and clock makers use Roman numerals to make their watches and clocks look good.

Show the numbers 3, 6, 9 and 12 using Roman numerals.

2 Kings and queens often use Roman numerals in their names.

Why?

King Louis XIV of France ruled from 1643 to 1715.
What number is XIV?

3 Roman numerals are sometimes used on tombstones.

(a) What do you think $\frac{8}{III}$ 1896 and $\frac{27}{VI}$ 1972 stand for?

R.I.P

_____

$\frac{8}{III}$ 1896 – $\frac{27}{VI}$ 1972

_____

(b) What does XIX stand for?

R.I.P

Departed

XIX September MDCC CVC

Complete Worksheet **1** – Page **171 – 172**

Writing Roman Numerals to 100

In Focus

We use place value and zero.

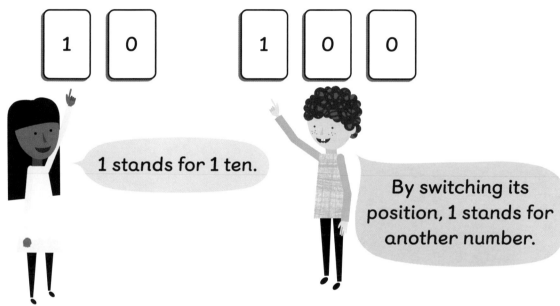

1 stands for 1 ten.

By switching its position, 1 stands for another number.

The Romans did not use place value or zero. When they needed a larger number, they used a new letter.

V = 5
L = 50

X = 10
C = 100

Find out how the Romans wrote the numbers 20, 30, 40 and so on.

1 Write the Roman numerals for 20, 30, 60, 70 and 80.

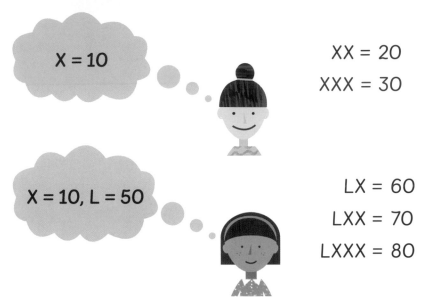

X = 10

XX = 20
XXX = 30

X = 10, L = 50

LX = 60
LXX = 70
LXXX = 80

2 Write the Roman numerals for 40 and 90.

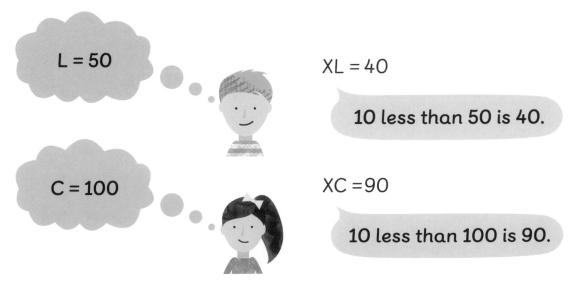

L = 50

XL = 40

10 less than 50 is 40.

C = 100

XC = 90

10 less than 100 is 90.

In Roman numerals, placing 10 before 50 makes 40.
Similarly, placing 10 before 100 makes 90.

Guided Practice

We still use the Roman numerals in Olympic Games.

1 London hosted the 4th, 14th and 30th Summer Olympic Games. Write 4, 14 and 30 in Roman numerals.

[   ] Olympic Summer Games

2 Tokyo is hosting the 32nd Summer Olympic Games. Write 32 in Roman numerals.

[   ] Olympic Summer Games

Complete Worksheet 2 – Page 173 – 175

Mind Workout

When the Roman numeral for 4 is seen in a mirror, it looks like 6.

IV | VI

These are some mirror images of numbers in Roman numerals.

| IIV | IX | IIXX | IVX | XIX |

What are the original numbers?

What do you notice about XIX? Are there other numbers like that?

The numerals we use in mathematics today are Hindu-Arabic numerals. Seventeen is written as 17.

The numerals we have learned in this chapter are Roman numerals. Seventeen is written as XVII.

Other cultures wrote numbers differently.
Find out about Mayan numerals, Chinese numerals and Thai numerals.

Let's do some research about them!

I know how to...

☐ read and write Roman numerals for 1 to 20.

☐ read and write Roman numerals to 100.

Self Check